D1102032

MRCP

New 'Best of Five'

Multiple Choice

Revision Book

PASTEST
Dedicated to your success

MRCP 1

New 'Best of Five'

Multiple Choice

Revision Book

Khalid Binymin

MBChB MRCP MSc
Consultant Physician and Rheumatologist
Southport and Formby General Hospital
Southport

PASTEST
Dedicated to your success

© 2002 PASTEST LTD
Egerton Court
Parkgate Estate
Knutsford
Cheshire WA16 8DX

Telephone: 01565 752000

All rights reserved. No part of this publication may be reproduced, stored in a retrieval system, or transmitted, in any form or by any means, electronic, mechanical, photocopying, recording or otherwise without the prior permission of the copyright owner.

First published 2002
Reprinted 2002

ISBN 1 901198 57 X

A catalogue record for this book is available from the British Library.

The information contained within this book was obtained by the author from reliable sources. However, while every effort has been made to ensure its accuracy, no responsibilty for loss, damage or injury occasioned to any person acting or refraining from action as a result of information contained herein can be accepted by the publishers or author.

PasTest Revision Books and Intensive Courses
PasTest has been established in the field of postgraduate medical education since 1972, providing revision books and intensive study courses for doctors preparing for their professional examinations.
Books and courses are available for the following specialties:
MRCP Part 1 and Part 2, MRCPCH Part 1 and Part 2, MRCOG, DRCOG, MRCGP, MRCPsych, DCH, FRCA, MRCS, PLAB.
For further details contact:
**PasTest, Freepost, Knutsford, Cheshire WA16 7BR
Tel: 01565 752000   Fax: 01565 650264
E-mail: enquiries@pastest.co.uk
Web site: www.pastest.co.uk**

Typeset by Breeze Ltd, Manchester.
Printed by MPG Books Ltd, Bodmin, Cornwall.

CONTENTS

ACKNOWLEDGEMENTS

S Almond   Consultant, Acute Medical Unit, Royal Liverpool Hospital, Liverpool.

N Kennedy   Consultant Physician in Infectious Diseases, Monklands Hospital, Airdrie.

B Maher   Snr Registrar in Medicine, Royal Liverpool Hospital, Liverpool.

P Murray   Respiratory SpR, (Rotation) North East Thames, London.

H Paynter   Formerly SpR Renal Medicine, Gloucestershire Royal Hospital, Gloucester.

K Smyth   Consultant Ophthalmologist, Royal Bolton Hospital, Bolton.

A Wade   Senior Lecturer in Medical Statistics, Department of Epidemiology and Public Health, Institute of Child Health, London.

PREFACE

This new book has been published at a time of great change in medicine and in the Membership examination. From May 2002 the MRCP 1 examination will change in format. There will be 2 papers each of two and a half hours duration.

Paper 1:60 multiple true/false questions with 300 individual items
Paper 2:100 multiple choice 'best of five' questions (there is one best
          answer)

Negative marking will be discontinued and the examination will be criterion referenced i.e. there will be a pre-determined pass mark.

This subject-based book of 300 new questions in the **'best of five'** format will be an invaluable tool, providing a complete and comprehensive review of medical topics relevant to all candidates who wish to practise the new style questions. The material contained in the book is based on recent advances in medicine with significant emphasis on basic sciences. The questions are interesting, testing, imaginative and also include expanded and detailed up-to-date teaching notes to aid revision. The subject based chapters reflect the actual exam syllabus content to test your knowledge and highlight weak areas for further revision.

I would like to thank all colleagues at Southport District General Hospital and Hope Hospital, Manchester who helped with reviewing the material for this book.

Good luck with your revision

Khalid Binymin

1: BASIC SCIENCES

1.1 When evaluating a patient with isolated enlarged inguinal lymph nodes, which one of the following areas is the LEAST likely site that warrants thorough examination?

- ❏ A Perineum
- ❏ B Testes
- ❏ C Uterus
- ❏ D External genitalia
- ❏ E Feet

1.2 Abnormal apoptosis is least implicated in the pathogenesis of which one of the following conditions?

- ❏ A Systemic lupus erythematosus
- ❏ B Alzheimer's disease
- ❏ C Ischaemic heart disease
- ❏ D Lung cancer
- ❏ E Myelodysplastic syndrome

1.3 Which one of the following is true about cytokines?

- ❏ A Cytokines are exclusively produced by immune system cells
- ❏ B Interleukin-6 (IL-6) enhances albumin synthesis by the liver
- ❏ C Interleukin-2 (IL-2) is derived from wandering macrophages
- ❏ D Th1 cells regulate allergic reaction and antibody production
- ❏ E Transforming growth factor-beta (TGF-beta) inhibits other cytokine production

1.4 Which one of the following is NOT true about seminal fluid?

- ❏ A Semen is produced in the testes and stored in the seminal vesicle
- ❏ B In a human it takes approximately three months for complete maturation of a sperm
- ❏ C Normally up to 20% of the sperms in an ejaculate are abnormal
- ❏ D Sperm concentration may be temporarily suppressed by fever
- ❏ E Sildenafil (*Viagra*) doubles the sperm count three months after the initiation of treatment

1.5 **Each of the following factors stimulate the release of renin EXCEPT?**

❏ A Assumption of the erect posture
❏ B Overactive sympathetic adrenergic neurones
❏ C Salt depletion
❏ D Prostaglandins
❏ E Angiotensin II

1.6 **Which one of the following muscles in the hand is supplied by the median nerve?**

❏ A Lateral two interossei
❏ B Abductor pollicis brevis
❏ C Medial two lumbricales
❏ D Flexor pollicis longus
❏ E Extensor pollicis

1.7 **Which one of the following statements is NOT true regarding vasopressin?**

❏ A Synthesised in the posterior pituitary
❏ B Makes distal convoluted tubules more permeable to hypotonic fluid
❏ C Increases circulating factor VIII and von Willebrand factor concentration
❏ D Stimulates ACTH release by the pituitary
❏ E Induces vasoconstriction in splanchnic vessels

1.8 **Which one of the following cells is NOT a tissue macrophage?**

❏ A Osteoblasts
❏ B Microglial cells (CNS)
❏ C Kupffer cells
❏ D Mesangial cells (kidney)
❏ E Endothelial cells

1.9   Acclimatisation to high altitude involves each of the following changes EXCEPT?

❏   A   Alveolar hypoventilation
❏   B   Reduced plasma volume
❏   C   Raised haematocrit
❏   D   Increased renal excretion of bicarbonate
❏   E   Increased pulmonary perfusion

1.10   The blood buffers include each of the following EXCEPT?

❏   A   Bicarbonate
❏   B   Sulphate
❏   C   Protein
❏   D   Haemoglobin
❏   E   Phosphate

1.11   Which one of the following is MOST likely to increase during exercise?

❏   A   Peripheral vascular resistance
❏   B   Pulmonary vascular resistance
❏   C   Stroke volume
❏   D   Diastolic pressure
❏   E   Venous compliance

1.12   Which one of the following is NOT accurate about hyponatraemia?

❏   A   In heart failure it indicates poor prognosis
❏   B   In liver cirrhosis it is due to reduced free water excretion
❏   C   With normal osmolality paraproteinaemia should be considered
❏   D   In the presence of high urea and high serum potassium it is suggestive of Addison's disease
❏   E   Confusion and coma often ensue when serum sodium approaches 125 mmol/l

1.13 **Which one of the following is higher at the apex of the lung than at the base when a person is standing?**

❏ A V/Q ratio
❏ B Ventilation
❏ C PaCO$_2$
❏ D Compliance
❏ E Blood flow

1.14 **The primary neurochemical disturbance in idiopathic Parkinson's disease involves**

❏ A Noradrenaline
❏ B Dopamine
❏ C Gamma-aminobutyric acid (GABA)
❏ D Substance P
❏ E Adrenaline

1.15 **Which one of the following pathological features is pathognomonic of the disease listed below?**

❏ A Reed-Sternberg cells in Hodgkin's disease
❏ B Aschoff nodules in rheumatic fever
❏ C Charcot-Leyden crystals in sputum from patient with asthma
❏ D Alcoholic hyaline (Mallory body) from liver biopsy specimen in alcoholic liver disease
❏ E Non-caseating granuloma in sarcoidosis

1.16 **The secretion of growth hormone is increased by?**

❏ A Hyperglycaemia
❏ B Exercise
❏ C Somatostatin
❏ D Growth hormone
❏ E Free fatty acids

1.17 **Which one of the following malignant tumours has the highest predilection for dissemination to bone?**

❏   A   Breast
❏   B   Prostate
❏   C   Kidney
❏   D   Lung
❏   E   Thyroid

1.18 **Which one of the following statements regarding cerebrospinal fluid (CSF) is true?**

❏   A   It is absorbed by the choroid plexus
❏   B   It circulates in the epidural space
❏   C   It has a lower glucose concentration than plasma
❏   D   It has a higher protein concentration than plasma
❏   E   It diffuses along the nerves back into the blood circulation

1.19 **Aldosterone secretion is stimulated by each of the following EXCEPT?**

❏   A   Angiotensin II
❏   B   ACTH
❏   C   Hyponatraemia
❏   D   Hyperkalaemia
❏   E   Renin

1.20 **The following statements are true about tumour necrosis factor (TNF) EXCEPT?**

❏   A   It inhibits angiogenesis hence the prominent anti-tumour activity
❏   B   It increases vascular permeability and promotes inflammation
❏   C   It recruits leucocytes to the site by inducing adhesion molecules
❏   D   It is produced primarily by activated monocytes and macrophages
❏   E   Anti-TNF-α therapies reduce inflammation and inhibit the progression of rheumatoid arthritis

1.21 **Vasoconstriction in response to hypoxia readily occurs in each of the following vascular beds EXCEPT?**

❏ A Bowel
❏ B Stomach
❏ C Cutaneous
❏ D Skeletal muscle
❏ E Coronary

1.22 **Each of the following is true regarding the diaphragm EXCEPT?**

❏ A Composed of smooth involuntary muscle and central tendon
❏ B Innervated by the phrenic nerve
❏ C Normally the right hemi-diaphragm is higher than the left one
❏ D When paralysed it moves upward
❏ E Hiccough is due to spasmodic contraction of the diaphragm

1.23 **A 69-year-old man presents with acute confusion. He has lost 8 kilograms in weight in the last two months. Blood tests reveal serum calcium levels of 3 mmol/l and a significantly elevated parathyroid hormone-related hormone (PTH-rP) . The tumour cell type most probably responsible for this disorder is?**

❏ A Neuroendocrine
❏ B Squamous
❏ C Large cell
❏ D Mesenchymal
❏ E Columnar

1.24 **Which one of the following is TRUE regarding the complement system?**

❏ A IgA activates the classical complement pathway
❏ B Hereditary angioedema is associated with C1 complement deficiency
❏ C Hypocomplementaemia is often an early feature of scleroderma renal disease
❏ D Homozygous C2 deficiency is associated with systemic lupus erythematosus
❏ E Homozygous C7 deficiency is associated with increased susceptibility to HIV infections

1.25 **Leptin is a hormone responsible for regulating fat mass in the body. Which one of the following statements regarding this hormone is TRUE?**

❏ A   It is secreted by the pancreas
❏ B   It acts directly on adipocytes in the subcutaneous tissue and causes proliferation of fat cells
❏ C   The vast majority of obese individuals have markedly elevated plasma leptin concentrations
❏ D   It enhances appetite
❏ E   It suppresses energy expenditure

1.26 **High potassium intake has all the following beneficial effects EXCEPT?**

❏ A   Lowers blood pressure in both hypertensive and normotensive individuals
❏ B   Reduces the risk of stroke
❏ C   Reduces urinary calcium excretion, which reduces the risk of kidney stones
❏ D   Prevents bone demineralisation
❏ E   Lowers high blood cholesterol

1.27 **Which one of the following represents the recommended daily dietary intake of calcium and vitamin D in the treatment of established osteoporosis?**

❏ A   800 mg/day of calcium, 100 µg/day of vitamin D
❏ B   1500 mg/day of calcium, 400–800 µg/day of vitamin D
❏ C   1200 mg/day of calcium, 200–400 µg/day of vitamin D
❏ D   900 mg/day of calcium, 200 µg/day of vitamin D
❏ E   1800 mg/day of calcium, 800–1000 µg/day of vitamin D

1.28 **Which one of the following statements is TRUE with regard to immunoglobulins?** FALSE

❏ A   IgA immunoglobulins cross the placenta
❏ B   IgG has the highest molecular weight in plasma
❏ C   IgM has the highest concentration in plasma
❏ D   All immunoglobulins except IgG are synthesised in the liver
❏ E   Levels are typically normal in Di George syndrome

1.29 **Cyclo-oxygenase-2 (COX-2) enzyme inhibition results in each of the following effects EXCEPT?**

❏ A Anti-inflammatory
❏ B Anti-platelet
❏ C Analgesic
❏ D Sodium retention
❏ E Bronchospasm

1.30 **Each of the following cellular pathophysiological processes occurs in the shock state EXCEPT?**

❏ A Increase in sodium/potassium ATPase activity
❏ B Cellular swelling
❏ C Precipitation of calcium in the mitochondria
❏ D Increase in insulin-mediated glucose uptake in muscle
❏ E Depletion of ATP and cyclic AMP

2: CARDIOLOGY

2.1   **Which one of the following statements BEST describes primary pulmonary hypertension?**

- ❏ A   The familial form is inherited as sex-linked recessive
- ❏ B   Chronic thromboembolic disease can be identified in 30% of primary cases
- ❏ C   Spontaneous remission is the rule in more than half the cases
- ❏ D   Cannabis inhalation may induce similar disease
- ☑ E   The mean pulmonary artery pressure is more than 25 mmHg at rest

2.2   **Paradoxical splitting of the second heart sound is not a feature in which one of the following conditions?**

- ❏ A   Atrial septal defect (ASD)
- ❏ B   Aortic stenosis
- ❏ C   Left bundle branch block (LBBB)
- ❏ D   Type B Wolff-Parkinson-White syndrome (WPW)
- ❏ E   Patent ductus arteriosus (PDA)

2.3   **Which one of the following features is MOST typical of coarctation of the aorta?**

- ❏ A   The coarctation is proximal to the left subclavian artery origin if the right arm blood pressure is significantly higher than in the left arm
- ❏ B   Continuous murmur over the thoracic spine usually originates from extensive collaterals
- ❏ C   Rib notching on plain chest X-ray can be identified as early as three months after birth
- ❏ D   Atrial septal defect (ASD) is the commonest associated congenital abnormality
- ❏ E   The risk for subacute bacterial endocarditis is low and antibiotic prophylaxis is seldom required

2.4   Which one of the following is characteristic of atrial myxoma?

❏   A   Usually originates in the right atrium
❏   B   Fragments of tumour easily break off and grow in its peripheral sites
❏   C   Echocardiogram is diagnostic in most cases
☑   D   The clinical signs can mimic severe mitral regurgitation
❏   E   Recurrence is frequent even after successful surgical removal of the tumour

2.5   Which one of the following is true regarding subacute bacterial endocarditis (SBE)?

❏   A   The risk of infection for mitral valve lesions is higher than for aortic valve lesions
❏   B   Q fever is the most frequent cause of culture negative endocarditis
❏   C   If *Streptococcus bovis* endocarditis is diagnosed a thorough investigation of the colon is indicated
❏   D   In early prosthetic valve endocarditis *Staphylococcus aureus* is frequently isolated
❏   E   Prophylaxis for endocarditis is probably not required to cover cystoscopy

2.6   Prolonged QT interval is a recognised complication of each of the following EXCEPT?

❏   A   Quinidine therapy
❏   B   Hypokalaemia
❏   C   Tricyclic antidepressant therapy
❏   D   Amiodarone therapy
❏   E   Digoxin therapy

2.7   Each of the following is typical of acute bacterial endocarditis EXCEPT?

❏   A   *Staphylococcus aureus* is the most frequent causative agent
❏   B   Large vegetation
❏   C   Affects normal as well as damaged heart valves
❏   D   Metastatic abscess is a recognised feature
❏   E   Cardiac conduction defect is often due to acute coronary insufficiency

2.8   A 57-year-old female is admitted with Gram-negative septicaemia. She is given intravenous antibiotics and normal saline. Two days later she becomes anxious, tachypnoeic, and short of breath. An emergency chest X-ray demonstrates diffuse, bilateral interstitial and alveolar infiltrates. Her past medical history revealed hypertension and that she has been on regular antihypertensive treatment for seven years. She has never had any evidence of congestive heart failure. In this case, adult respiratory distress syndrome can be distinguished from cardiogenic pulmonary oedema by?

❏   A   Measurement of the central venous pressure
❏   B   Calculation of the alveolar-arterial pO_2 difference
❏   C   Measurement of pulmonary artery wedge pressure
❏   D   Measurement of lung compliance
❏   E   Measurement of ejection fraction

2.9   A 30-year-old woman presents with a three month history of chest pain. On auscultation, there is a midsystolic click and a late systolic murmur. Her electrocardiogram shows T-wave inversions in leads II, III, and aVF. Which of the following statements concerning her condition is true?

❏   A   The woman's chest pain could be due to associated coronary artery disease
❏   B   The click and murmur occur later in systole when the patient stands
❏   C   An exercise stress test would most likely be positive
❏   D   Asymmetrical hypertrophy of the interventricular septum is revealed on echocardiography
❏   E   Prophylactic measures to prevent subacute bacterial endocarditis are not warranted

2.10   Aortic stenosis in adults is commonly the result of which one of the following?

❏   A   Bicuspid aortic valve disease
❏   B   Left ventricular membrane
❏   C   Hypertrophic obstructive cardiomyopathy (HOCM)
❏   D   Rheumatic fever
❏   E   Cystic medial necrosis

2.11 **Left bundle branch block is associated with which one of the following conditions?**

❑   A   Ischaemic heart disease
❑   B   Mitral stenosis
❑   C   Pericarditis
❑   D   Pulmonary embolism
❑   E   Tricuspid stenosis

2.12 **One of the following statements is true regarding subacute bacterial endocarditis (SBE)?**

❑   A   Absent cardiac murmur at presentation virtually excludes the diagnosis of SBE
❑   B   The spleen is often enlarged and usually tender
❑   C   Glomerulonephritis is due to autoimmune mechanism
❑   D   Mycotic aneurysms most frequently affect medium sized renal arteries
❑   E   Heart failure when present is usually mild and does not affect the outcome

2.13 **Normal pregnancy is associated with which one of the following haemodynamic changes?**

❑   A   A 20% reduction in blood volume and cardiac output
❑   B   A 10 mmHg drop in diastolic blood pressure toward the end of pregnancy
❑   C   Bradycardia with a radial pulse rate between 45 and 55 beats per minute
❑   D   Grade 2/6 diastolic murmur at the mitral area
❑   E   Pulsus alternans

2.14	A 55-year-old Afro-American businessman attends the outpatient clinic with pain in his legs. On examination, his left arm blood pressure is 160/110 mmHg and the right arm is 130/80 mmHg. Regular blood pressure readings remain constant three months later. The peripheral pulses are unequal in the arms. Which of the following statements is NOT true?

❏	A	This patient is hypertensive
❏	B	The arm with the highest mean blood pressure reading should be used for BP measurement
❏	C	A rise in diastolic pressure when the patient goes from the supine to the standing position is most compatible with essential hypertension
❏	D	Ambulatory blood pressure monitoring is necessary for further treatment monitoring
❏	E	Beta-blockers may not be effective in controlling the blood pressure

2.15	In the evaluation of venous thromboembolism (VTE), which one of the following is true of plasma D-dimer testing?

❏	A	It has high sensitivity, so a positive test establishes the diagnosis in most patients
❏	B	It is usually negative when pulmonary embolism is confined to sub-segmental vessels
❏	C	It is positive only in VTE
❏	D	It can reliably distinguish between ruptured Baker's cyst and deep venous thrombosis
❏	E	It has high negative predictive values, so a negative result completely excludes VTE

2.16	Regarding acute aortic regurgitation, which one of the following is true?

❏	A	Rheumatic fever is the most frequent cause
❏	B	The pulse pressure is wider than in chronic aortic regurgitation
❏	C	The fourth heart sound S4 is often present
❏	D	Left ventricular dilatation is a helpful early echocardiographic finding
❏	E	It is often regarded as a medical emergency

2.17 **A 60-year-old man underwent a coronary angiogram for unstable angina. The next day whilst recovering in hospital he complains of severe pain in his right foot and partial loss of sight in the left eye. On examination the lower limb peripheral pulses are present and of good volume. There is gangrene of the lateral two toes on the right foot. Fundoscopy reveals cholesterol emboli in a branch of the central retinal artery in the left eye. Which one of the following is the most probable diagnosis in this case?**

- ☑ A Atheroembolic disease
- ☐ B Polyarteritis nodosa
- ☐ C Buerger's disease
- ☐ D Arterial thromboembolism
- ☐ E Disseminated intravascular coagulopathy

2.18 **Which one of the following features is MORE common in constrictive pericarditis than in cardiac tamponade?**

- ☐ A Pulsus paradoxus
- ☐ B Kussmaul's sign
- ☐ C Prominent x trough
- ☐ D 4-chamber diastolic equilibrium
- ☐ E Right-sided heart failure

3: CLINICAL PHARMACOLOGY AND TOXICOLOGY

3.1 **Which one of the following features is MOST characteristic of lead poisoning?**

- ❑ A Predominantly sensory peripheral neuropathy
- ❑ B Posterior uveitis
- ❑ C Punctuate basophilic stippling on peripheral blood film examination
- ❑ D Membranous glomerulonephritis as the primary kidney lesion
- ❑ E A gingival blue line in children

3.2 **D-penicillamine is an antidote used as a chelating agent for which one of the following heavy metal poisoning?**

- ❑ A Thallium
- ❑ B Copper
- ❑ C Arsenic
- ❑ D Lead
- ❑ E Mercury

3.3 **A 31-year-old pregnant woman, was found by her husband in the garage cyanosed and agitated. Apparently she left the car engine running while she was clearing the garage before driving to her maternity hospital appointment. She smokes heavily but has no previous medical problems. She was rushed to the accident and emergency department. On arrival it was thought that she had carbon monoxide (CO) poisoning. Which one of the following statements is NOT true?**

- ❑ A The baseline CO may exceed 15% in smokers as compared with 1–3% in non-smokers
- ❑ B The affinity of haemoglobin for CO is 200–250 times as great as its affinity for oxygen
- ❑ C The final CO level in the fetus may significantly exceed the levels in the mother
- ❑ D Venous blood samples are adequate for measurements of CO in the blood
- ❑ E CT scan of the brain identifies hypodense periventricular lesions characteristic of CO poisoning

3.4 **A 20-year-old student is admitted with collapse. He was with friends and was upset about his final examination result. They mentioned that he had a lot to drink and probably took an overdose of an unknown substance. On examination he smells of alcohol and is comatose. The pupils are small but there are no localising signs. The full blood count, glucose, urea and electrolyte, liver function test and INR are all within normal limits. He is intubated and given naloxone intravenously. He becomes more alert but starts to experience abdominal cramps, nausea and vomiting. Regarding this patient which one of the following statements is NOT correct?**

❏ A   Naloxone reverses the CNS toxicity of ethanol (alcohol)
❏ B   The patient is probably an opioid addict
❏ C   Plasma paracetamol concentration should be measured urgently
❏ D   Naloxone is the only specific opioid antagonist which reverses the effect of all opioids
❏ E   When venous access is not possible naloxone can be introduced down the endotracheal tube

3.5 **Which one of the following antimicrobial drugs has the LEAST anti-anaerobic activity?**

❏ A   Clindamycin
❏ B   Amoxycillin
❏ C   Gentamycin
❏ D   Tetracycline
❏ E   Chloramphenicol

3.6 **Which one of the following statements BEST describes warfarin?**

❏ A   Reduces protein C levels in the blood
❏ B   It may induce autoimmune thrombocytopenia
❏ C   Chronic use is often associated with osteoporosis
❏ D   An initial loading dose is given because it has a short half-life (3 hours)
❏ E   Should be avoided in lactating women

3.7   **Each of the following is true about vancomycin EXCEPT?**

- ❏   A   Inhibits bacterial DNA replication
- ❏   B   Has no significant effect on Gram-negative cocci
- ❏   C   Poorly absorbed when given by mouth
- ❏   D   Eliminated mainly by the kidney
- ❏   E   Ototoxicity is the main side-effect

3.8   **Which one of the following diuretics is associated with metabolic acidosis?**

- ❏   A   Bumetanide
- ❏   B   Metolazone
- ❏   C   Thiazide
- ❏   D   Frusemide
- ❏   E   Acetazolamide

3.9   **Metformin therapy is associated with all of the following effects EXCEPT?**

- ❏   A   Reduces absorption of carbohydrates from the gut
- ❏   B   Stimulates the pancreas to release stored insulin
- ❏   C   Reduces hepatic gluconeogenesis
- ❏   D   Clinical hypoglycaemia is rare
- ❏   E   Increases the utilisation of glucose in peripheral tissues

3.10   **Which one of the following statements is true about SSRIs when compared with tricyclic antidepressant?**

- ❏   A   More sedative effect
- ❏   B   Weight gain is a recognised side-effect
- ❏   C   Less profound antimuscarinic effect
- ❏   D   Safely used in epilepsy
- ❏   E   Drug free period is not necessary when prescribed to replace monoamino oxidase inhibitors (MAOI)

3.11 **Which one of the following statements BEST describes radioactive iodine (^{131}I) in the treatment of thyrotoxicosis?**

❏ A Triple dose therapy (one month apart) is the standard regimen used in most cases

❏ B Given by intravenous infusion to avoid gastrointestinal toxicity

❏ C Not associated with increased incidence of late leukaemia

❏ D Hypoparathyroidism secondary to beta-emissions and ablation of the parathyroid gland occurs in 30% of cases

❏ E Rapid regression of exophthalmos is expected in almost all cases within the first three months

3.12 **Which one of the following statements is NOT accurate about drug-induced liver disease?**

❏ A Isoniazid (INH) typically causes liver damage in fast acetylators

❏ B Halothane hepatitis usually becomes evident approximately seven to ten days after anaesthesia

❏ C Erythromycin stearate can cause cholestasis

❏ D Phenytoin characteristically produces liver granuloma

❏ E Aspirin in excess of 3 grams per day causes chronic hepatitis

3.13 **Which one of the following antiplatelet agents acts by inhibiting the phosphodiesterase enzyme and increasing the cellular concentration of cyclic adenosine monophosphate (cAMP)?**

❏ A Abciximab

❏ B Ticlopidine

❏ C Aspirin

❏ D Clopidogrel

❏ E Dipyridamole

3.14 **β-blockers (β-adrenergic agents) are used in the treatment of angina because they have one of the following properties?**

❏ A Increase sinus node automaticity

❏ B Increase the left atrial volume and pressure

❏ C Increase the peripheral vascular resistance

❏ D Decrease the heart rate and myocardial contractility

❏ E Increase the preload

3.15 **A 40-year-old obese female teacher is determined to lose weight. She exercises three times a week at the local gym and is on a slimming diet. In the last month she managed to lose three kilograms in weight and asked your opinion about initiating Orlistat therapy. On advising her you would explain that Orlistat therapy has which one of the following effects?**

- ❏ A Prevents fat absorption from the intestine
- ❏ B Improves the bone mineral density
- ❏ C Causes dramatic weight loss in the first month
- ❏ D Increases the cholesterol level in the first year of therapy
- ❏ E Increases the risk of clotting

3.16 **Propylthiouracil has a modest therapeutic advantage over carbimazole in the treatment of thyrotoxicosis because it has which one of the following properties?**

- ❏ A Inhibits the organification of iodine at the thyroid gland
- ❏ B Is not excreted in breast milk
- ❏ C Is more potent
- ❏ D Has different chemical structure and hence does not share the same adverse effects profile
- ❏ E Inhibits T4 to T3 conversion

3.17 **Which one of the following cytotoxic agents is frequently associated with cardiotoxicity?**

- ❏ A Doxorubicin
- ❏ B Cyclophosphamide
- ❏ C Cisplatin
- ❏ D Bleomycin
- ❏ E Vincristine

3.18   A 65-year-old woman with type 2 diabetes of 11 years' duration presents with poorly controlled blood glucose levels. She was overweight and initially started on metformin therapy. Her diabetes was well controlled until the last 12 months. Despite strict adherence to diet, exercise and maximum daily doses of metformin, satisfactory blood glucose control has proved difficult to achieve and the last Hb A_{1c} was at 13%. You consider adding pioglitazone. This agent is which one of the following?

❏   A   A benzoic acid derivative
❏   B   An α-glucosidase inhibitor
❏   C   An insulin secretagogue which stimulates insulin secretion by the beta cell
❏   D   A sulphonylurea
❏   E   An insulin sensitizer which decreases peripheral insulin resistance

3.19   Which one of the following antihypertensive agents controls the blood pressure by blocking the peripheral α_1-adrenoceptor?

❏   A   Losartan
❏   B   Doxazosin
❏   C   Minoxidil
❏   D   Methyldopa
❏   E   Clonidine

3.20   Which one of the following contributes to the beneficial effect of nitro-glycerine?

❏   A   Decreases oxygen transport to the myocardium
❏   B   Dilation of systemic veins
❏   C   Increase of left ventricular preload
❏   D   Reduces sodium potassium transport in myocardial muscle
❏   E   Increase of left ventricular afterload

3.21   Each of the following regarding cyclosporin A is true EXCEPT?

❏   A   It is an alkylating agent
❏   B   It acts primarily on T-helper lymphocyte
❏   C   Ketoconazole inhibits its hepatic metabolism
❏   D   Myelosuppression is not an adverse effect often encountered
         with cyclosporin therapy
❏   E   Hirsutism is usually reversible after cessation of treatment

3.22   Which one of the following is true regarding amiodarone?

❏   A   5% of its weight is iodine
❏   B   It causes shortening of the QT intervals
❏   C   It has calcium channel blocking properties
❏   D   It has no effect on potassium channels
❏   E   It promotes renal excretion of digoxin when used concomitantly

**3.23   Which one of the following anticonvulsants has been associated
         with the development of polycystic ovarian syndrome (PCO)?**

❏   A   Vigabatrin
❏   B   Sodium valproate
❏   C   Phenobarbitone
❏   D   Phenytoin
❏   E   Topiramate

**3.24   Which one of the following is not a recognised treatment for
         acromegaly?**

❏   A   Somatostatin analogues
❏   B   Bromocriptine
❏   C   Octreotide
❏   D   Somatotropin
❏   E   Cabergoline

3.25   With respect to inhaled intrapulmonary delivery of insulin, which one of the following is true?

❏   A   Cigarette smoking has no effect on absorption of inhaled insulin
❏   B   Abolishes the need for subcutaneous insulin injections in type I diabetes
❏   C   10–30% of the inhaled dose of insulin is absorbed into the circulation
❏   D   When used alone offers adequate glycaemic control for Type I diabetes
❏   E   Results in a deterioration in pulmonary function

3.26   Which one of the following pharmacokinetic parameters remains normal in chronic renal failue?

❏   A   Absorption
❏   B   Protein binding
❏   C   Volume of distribution
❏   D   Renal metabolism of drugs
❏   E   Bioavailability immediately following intravenous injection of a drug

3.27   In renal drug elimination, the extraction ratio can be defined as which one of the following?

❏   A   Decline of drug concentration in the plasma from the arterial to the venous side of the kidney
❏   B   A measure of the time during which the concentration of drug in the plasma falls by 50%
❏   C   The proportion of an orally administered drug reaching the circulation
❏   D   The ratio of drug concentration in the urine to drug concentration in the bile
❏   E   The concentration of a drug in the urine divided by the concentration in the plasma

3.28   Which one of the following is associated with hyperkalaemia?

❏   A   Bartter's syndrome
❏   B   Treatment with corticosteroids
❏   C   Liquorice addiction
❏   D   Liddle's syndrome
❏   E   Cyclosporin

3.29   **Which one of the following treatments is effective in severe lithium toxicity?**

❑   A   Activated charcoal
❑   B   Methionine
❑   C   Haemodialysis
❑   D   Forced diuresis with sodium chloride
❑   E   Methylprednisolone

3.30   **In relation to acute interstitial nephritis, which one of the following statements is INCORRECT?**

❑   A   Bilaterally large kidneys are typically seen on ultrasound scan
❑   B   The condition is immune mediated
❑   C   Allopurinol is a known cause
❑   D   Haematuria is a feature
❑   E   Renal function almost always remains normal

4: DERMATOLOGY

4.1 **Which one of the following conditions is LEAST likely to be associated with pyoderma gangrenosum?**

- ❏ A Tuberculosis
- ❏ B Rheumatoid arthritis
- ❏ C Chronic myeloid leukaemia
- ❏ D Ulcerative colitis
- ❏ E Lymphoma

4.2 **Vitiligo is associated with each of the following disorders EXCEPT?**

- ❏ A Nelson's syndrome
- ❏ B Alopecia areata
- ❏ C Graves' disease
- ❏ D Addison's disease
- ❏ E Diabetes mellitus

4.3 **Which one of the following disorders is MOST commonly associated with Stevens-Johnson syndrome?**

- ❏ A Herpes simplex infection
- ❏ B Sarcoidosis
- ❏ C Systemic lupus erythematosus
- ❏ D Herpes zoster infection
- ❏ E Coeliac disease

4.4 **Which one of the following disorders is LEAST associated with photosensitivity?**

- ❏ A Quinidine therapy
- ❏ B Discoid lupus
- ❏ C Acute intermittent porphyria
- ❏ D Pellagra
- ❏ E Systemic lupus erythematosus

4.5   **Koebner phenomenon is encountered in each of the following EXCEPT?**

❑   A   Pemphigus vulgaris
❑   B   Lichen planus
❑   C   Vitiligo
❑   D   Molluscum contagiosum
❑   E   Herpes simplex

5: ENDOCRINOLOGY AND METABOLIC DISORDERS

5.1 Which one of the following statements is incorrect regarding phaeochromocytoma?

- ❑ A Bilateral in 10% of cases
- ❑ B Malignant in 10% of cases
- ❑ C Extra-adrenal in 10% of cases
- ❑ D Extra-adrenal phaeochromocytomas secrete adrenaline
- ❑ E Familial cases almost always arise from the adrenal medulla

5.2 In patients with hypertension, the presence of hypokalaemia should prompt investigations of each of the following disorders EXCEPT?

- ❑ A Renal artery stenosis
- ❑ B Liddle's syndrome
- ❑ C Conn's syndrome
- ❑ D Cushing's syndrome
- ❑ E Bartter's syndrome

5.3 Which one of the following is LEAST associated with metabolic alkalosis?

- ❑ A Thiazide therapy
- ❑ B Frusemide therapy
- ❑ C Conn's syndrome
- ❑ D Addison's disease
- ❑ E Persistent vomiting

5.4 The presence of galactorrhoea is MOST suggestive of which one of the following conditions?

- ❑ A Turner's syndrome
- ❑ B Polycystic ovary disease
- ❑ C Myxoedema
- ❑ D Sheehan's syndrome
- ❑ E Bromocriptine therapy

5.5 **Which one of the following features is LEAST associated with thyrotoxicosis?**

❑ A   Diffuse swelling of the hands and feet
❑ B   Proximal myopathy
❑ C   Familial periodic paralysis
❑ D   Myasthenia gravis
❑ E   Peripheral neuropathy

5.6 **Which one of the following conditions is LEAST associated with hypoparathyroidism?**

❑ A   Addison's disease
❑ B   Di George syndrome
❑ C   Mucocutaneous candidiasis
❑ D   Medullary cell carcinoma
❑ E   Magnesium deficiency

5.7 **Which one of the following statements is true about Graves' disease and pregnancy?**

❑ A   Neonatal hyperthyroidism is unlikely if the maternal thyroxine level is strictly controlled during pregnancy
❑ B   Carbimazole is absolutely contraindicated
❑ C   Surgery can be safely conducted in the second trimester
❑ D   The presence of persistent exophthalmos indicates poor control of the active disease
❑ E   Anti-thyroid drugs do not enter breast milk

5.8 **Which one of the following conditions is LEAST associated with the syndrome of inappropriate antidiuretic hormone secretion (SIADH)?**

❑ A   Pneumococcal pneumonia
❑ B   Meningococcal meningitis
❑ C   Porphyria
❑ D   Sickle cell trait
❑ E   Vincristine therapy

5.9 **True statements describing gestational diabetes include each of the following EXCEPT?**

❑ A Usually resolve spontaneously after delivery
❑ B 5% will develop type II diabetes mellitus
❑ C Tends to recur in subsequent pregnancy
❑ D Associated with increased risk of fetal macrosomia
❑ E The risk of congenital malformation is not increased

5.10 **Hypophosphataemia is associated with each of the following potential complications EXCEPT?**

❑ A Haemolysis of red blood cells
❑ B Rhabdomyolysis
❑ C Encephalopathy
❑ D Metastatic calcification
❑ E Osteomalacia

5.11 **Which one of the following proteins is most likely to be associated with very high levels of plasma chylomicrons?**

❑ A Apoprotein E
❑ B Apoprotein CII
❑ C Apoprotein AII
❑ D Lipoprotein B
❑ E LDL receptor

5.12 **A 65-year-old woman known to have chronic low back pain notices severe sharp pain in the left groin after a minor fall and is unable to walk. Left neck of femur fracture is identified on radiological examination. Routine laboratory evaluation discloses a serum calcium concentration of 1.9 mmol/l, a serum phosphorus concentration of 0.78 mmol/l and increased serum alkaline phosphatase activity. The serum parathyroid hormone level was subsequently found to be elevated. The most likely diagnosis is?**

❑ A Primary hyperparathyroidism
❑ B Hypervitaminosis D
❑ C Paget's disease of bone
❑ D Osteoporosis
❑ E Vitamin D deficiency

5.13   Causes of hypokalaemia include each of the following EXCEPT?

❏   A   Metabolic alkalosis
❏   B   Renal tubular acidosis
❏   C   Gentamycin therapy
❏   D   Addison's disease
❏   E   Bartter's syndrome

5.14   Hypercalcaemia that usually responds to steroid therapy is a feature of each of the following disorders EXCEPT?

❏   A   Sarcoidosis
❏   B   Primary hyperparathyroidism
❏   C   Hypervitaminosis D
❏   D   Multiple myeloma
❏   E   Malignancy with bone metastases

5.15   Major causes of metabolic acidosis include each of the following EXCEPT?

❏   A   Chronic renal failure
❏   B   Methanol ingestion
❏   C   Conn's syndrome
❏   D   Parenteral hyperalimentation
❏   E   Prolonged therapy with amiloride

5.16   Each of the following features is characteristic of insulin resistance EXCEPT?

❏   A   Acanthosis nigricans
❏   B   Lipodystrophy
❏   C   Amenorrhoea and hirsutism
❏   D   Peripheral neuropathy
❏   E   Hypertension

5.17   In glucagonoma the MOST likely associated skin lesion is?

❏   A   Erythema chronicum migrans
❏   B   Acanthosis nigricans
❏   C   Panniculitis
❏   D   Ichthyosis
❏   E   Necrolytic migratory erythema

5.18 **A 56-year-old woman known to have hypothyroidism and currently taking thyroxine 100 mcg/day, is admitted to the orthopaedic unit with a left hip fracture after a fall at home. A bone mineral density (BMD) on the opposite femur confirms the diagnosis of osteoporosis with a T-score of -2.8. She was given alendronate   70 mg weekly. Each of the following statements is true EXCEPT?**

❏　A　Excessive thyroxine is an additional risk factor for osteoporosis
❏　B　Reduced bone density evident on plain radiography would only manifest when total bone density has decreased by 30–50%
❏　C　The T-score compares a patient's BMD with the mean value for persons of the same age and sex
❏　D　A low serum phosphate level may be suggestive of hyperparathyroidism
❏　E　Bisphosphonates such as alendronate act by inhibiting bone resorption

5.19 **Precocious puberty in boys is a feature of each of the following disorders EXCEPT?**

❏　A　Primary hypothyroidism
❏　B　Craniopharyngiomas
❏　C　Tuberous sclerosis
❏　D　Hepatoblastoma
❏　E　Gigantism

5.20 **In dietary deficiency each of the following statements is true EXCEPT?**

❏　A　Zinc deficiency causes acrodermatitis and altered taste
❏　B　Manganese deficiency is associated with persistent nausea
❏　C　Peripheral neuropathy and encephalopathy may result from chromium deficiency
❏　D　Copper deficiency causes Wilson' s disease
❏　E　Selenium deficiency causes haemolytic anaemia

5.21 **The following statements with regard to postpartum thyroiditis are true EXCEPT?**

❑ A Typically occurs in the first week after delivery
❑ B Characterised by transient hyperthyroidism
❑ C Spontaneous recovery is expected in 90% of cases
❑ D Anti-microsomal antibodies might be elevated
❑ E Radioactive iodine uptake is reduced

5.22 **Blood levels of high density lipoprotein are increased by which one of the following?**

❑ A Exercise
❑ B Alcohol
❑ C Oestrogen
❑ D Clofibrate therapy
❑ E Diabetes mellitus

6: GASTROENTEROLOGY

6.1 **Which one of the following statements BEST describes a person with irritable bowel syndrome (IBS)?**

- ❏ A Characterised by nocturnal diarrhoea
- ❏ B If there is nausea and vomiting the diagnosis should be reconsidered
- ❏ C Weight loss becomes more evident as the disease runs a chronic course
- ❏ D Sigmoidoscopy findings are often diagnostic
- ❏ E High fibre diet is often prescribed for the treatment of the syndrome

6.2 **Which one of the following pathological changes favours ulcerative colitis over Crohn's disease?**

- ❏ A Ileal involvement
- ❏ B Crypt abscesses
- ❏ C Transmural involvement
- ❏ D Granulomas
- ❏ E Skip lesions

6.3 **Which one of the following conditions is MOST likely to be associated with gastric acid hypersecretion?**

- ❏ A Pernicious anaemia
- ❏ B Large bowel resection
- ❏ C Vasoactive intestinal polypeptide (VIP)-secreting tumour
- ❏ D Systemic mastocytosis
- ❏ E Cushing's syndrome

6.4 **Which one of the following clinical findings is MOST characteristic of pseudomembranous colitis?**

- ❏ A Bloody diarrhoea, abdominal pain and tenderness
- ❏ B The detection of *Clostridium difficile* bacilli in the stools is diagnostic
- ❏ C The severe form of the disease is often associated with gentamycin therapy
- ❏ D Nosocomial outbreaks
- ❏ E Intravenous vancomycin for two weeks is an effective treatment

6.5   Jejunal biopsy is least helpful in establishing the diagnosis of which one of the following malabsorption syndromes?

❏ A   Coeliac disease
❏ B   Whipple's disease
❏ C   Eosinophilic gastroenteritis
❏ D   Intestinal lymphoma
❏ E   *Giardia lamblia*

6.6   Which one of the following statements regarding adenocarcinoma of the colon complicating ulcerative colitis is INCORRECT?

❏ A   Carcino-embryonic antigen (CEA) is not a reliable screening test
❏ B   The risk of carcinoma is higher if the colitis is confined to the left colon
❏ C   Mucosal dysplasia on rectal biopsy is associated with the likelihood of carcinoma elsewhere in the bowel
❏ D   It is multifocal in origin
❏ E   The prognosis is worse than colonic adenocarcinoma developing in the absence of colitis

6.7   Protein losing enteropathy is the LEAST likely manifestation of which one of the following disorders?

❏ A   Coeliac disease
❏ B   Cholera
❏ C   Whipple's disease
❏ D   Primary intestinal lymphangiectasia
❏ E   Ménétrièr's disease

6.8   Which one of the following clinical findings is MOST suggestive of amoebic liver abscess rather than pyogenic liver abscess?

❏ A   Patient usually more than 60 years old
❏ B   Recent bowel surgery
❏ C   Raised white cell count
❏ D   History of recent biliary colic and fever
❏ E   Solitary abscess in the right lobe of the liver

6.9 **Abnormal liver function with red cell haemolysis is LEAST likely to be encountered in which one of the following disorders?**

❑ A Diabetes mellitus
❑ B Treatment with methyldopa
❑ C Alcoholic hepatitis
❑ D *Mycoplasma pneumoniae*
❑ E Haemochromatosis

6.10 **Which one of the following clinical findings is true regarding carcinoid tumour?**

❑ A Most commonly found in the ileum
❑ B Carcinoid syndrome can manifest in the absence of liver metastases
❑ C Aortic stenosis is the most frequent heart valve disease in advanced carcinoid tumour
❑ D Carcinoid flush is often associated with an instant rise in diastolic blood pressure
❑ E Banana ingestion can block 5-HIAA renal clearance and give false negative test results

6.11 **Each of the following metabolic conditions is associated with increased incidence of primary hepatocellular carcinoma EXCEPT?**

❑ A Haemochromatosis
❑ B Hereditary tyrosinosis
❑ C Homozygous α_1-antitrypsin deficiency
❑ D Wilson's disease
❑ E Glycogen storage disease type 1

6.12   A 60-year-old male civil servant who is known to have
rheumatoid arthritis and is taking naproxen 500 mg/day is
found to have three duodenal ulcers and a 2 cm antral ulcer on
upper gastrointestinal endoscopy. Abdominal computed
tomography showed a 4 cm mass in the head of the pancreas.
The most probable diagnosis is?

❏ A   *H. pylori* induced multiple peptic ulcers
❏ B   Pancreatic lymphoma
❏ C   Glucagonoma
❏ D   NSAID-induced upper gastrointestinal ulcers
❏ E   Gastrinoma

6.13   Causes of acute pancreatitis include each of the following
EXCEPT?

❏ A   Alcoholism
❏ B   Polyarteritis nodosa
❏ C   Hyperlipidaemia
❏ D   Hypoparathyroidism
❏ E   Mumps

6.14   Which one of the following is true regarding liver function
tests?

❏ A   In human beings ALT (alanine aminotransferase) is exclusively
released from liver hepatocytes
❏ B   Hepatic synthesis of gamma globulin increases in chronic
autoimmune liver disease
❏ C   In the fasting state the esterification pathway is active to provide
energy
❏ D   A positive antimitochondrial antibody test virtually excludes bile
duct calculus as the cause of obstructive jaundice
❏ E   Ethanol induces hypoglycaemia by direct inhibition of
gluconeogenesis

6.15 **Each of the following conditions is known to cause fatty liver EXCEPT?**

- [ ] A Obesity
- [ ] B Corticosteroid therapy
- [ ] C Diabetes mellitus
- [ ] D Hypercholesterolaemia
- [ ] E Alcoholic liver disease

6.16 **Intestinal pseudo-obstruction is a recognised manifestation of each of the following disorders EXCEPT?**

- [ ] A Parkinson's disease
- [ ] B Scleroderma
- [ ] C Hyperthyroidism
- [ ] D Tricyclic antidepressant therapy
- [ ] E Idiopathic inherited as an autosomal dominant trait

6.17 **Which one of the following statements BEST describes liver diseases during pregnancy?**

- [ ] A Viral hepatitis runs a milder course
- [ ] B Acute fatty liver of pregnancy correlates with alcohol consumption prior to pregnancy
- [ ] C Asymptomatic rise of serum alkaline phosphatase warrants further investigations to exclude primary biliary cirrhosis
- [ ] D Cholestasis of pregnancy may recur in subsequent pregnancy
- [ ] E There is no evidence that hepatitis B virus can be transmitted vertically to the fetus

6.18 **Bilateral swelling of the parotid gland is rarely encountered in which one of the following conditions?**

- [ ] A Lymphoma
- [ ] B Alcoholic liver disease
- [ ] C Primary hypothyroidism
- [ ] D Sarcoidosis
- [ ] E Sjögren's syndrome

6.19 **Hepatic encephalopathy can be precipitated by each of the following conditions EXCEPT?**

❏ A Upper gastrointestinal bleeding
❏ B Hypokalaemia
❏ C Constipation
❏ D Diuretics
❏ E High carbohydrate diet

6.20 **Which one of the following disorders is MOST likely to be associated with _H. pylori_ infection?**

❏ A Non ulcer dyspepsia
❏ B Reflux oesophagitis
❏ C Coeliac disease
❏ D Gastric lymphoma
❏ E Achalasia of the cardia

6.21 **Which one of the following is accurate with regard to alcoholic liver disease?**

❏ A Men are more susceptible than women
❏ B In alcoholic hepatitis the aspartate aminotransferase to alanine aminotransferase (AST/ALT) ratio is 2:1
❏ C Hepatic iron overload is indicative of concomitant heterozygote haemochromatosis
❏ D Alcoholic fatty infiltration is irreversible once established
❏ E Unlike other causes of liver cirrhosis alcoholic cirrhosis does not progress to hepatoma

6.22 **Which one of the following hepatobiliary disorders is LEAST associated with jaundice during the course of the disease?**

❏ A Liver abscess
❏ B Acute viral hepatitis
❏ C Carcinoma of the head of the pancreas
❏ D Primary biliary cirrhosis
❏ E Alcoholic cirrhosis

6.23 **Conditions that predispose to colorectal cancer include each of the following EXCEPT?**

- ❏ A Ulcerative colitis
- ❏ B Crohn's disease
- ❏ C Uretero-sigmoid anastomosis
- ❏ D Intestinal tuberculosis
- ❏ E Familial adenomatous polyposis

6.24 **Which one of the following conditions is expected to be associated with normal urinary D-xylose test?**

- ❏ A Coeliac disease
- ❏ B Chronic pancreatitis
- ❏ C Blind loop syndrome
- ❏ D Chronic renal failure
- ❏ E Liver cirrhosis with ascites

6.25 **In a patient with liver cirrhosis which one of the listed features is characteristic of portal hypertension?**

- ❏ A Jaundice
- ❏ B Gynaecomastia
- ❏ C Spider telangiectases
- ❏ D Hepatomegaly
- ❏ E Oesophageal varices

6: Gastroenterology

7: GENETICS

7.1 **Which one of the following is LEAST characteristic of achondroplasia?**

❏ A   In most cases both parents are normal
❏ B   Endochondral ossification is defective
❏ C   Affects lower limb bones but spares upper limb bones
❏ D   Patients are usually fertile
❏ E   Hydrocephalus is a recognised feature

7.2 **Which one of the following is LEAST suggestive of Klinefelter's syndrome?**

❏ A   Karyotype 47,XXY
❏ B   Gynaecomastia
❏ C   The testes is firm on palpation
❏ D   Normal intelligence
❏ E   FSH and LH are elevated

7.3 **Which one of the following statements BEST describes a patient with Wilson's disease?**

❏ A   The primary defect is believed to be enhanced intestinal absorption of copper
❏ B   An alternative diagnosis should be considered if chorea occurs with no evidence of Kayser-Fleischer rings
❏ C   Chronic liver disease and autoimmune haemolytic anaemia are recognised features
❏ D   Raised serum copper levels evident at birth
❏ E   Siblings with biochemical evidence of the disease are treated only when they become symptomatic

7.4 **Each of the following diseases has an autosomal dominant inheritance EXCEPT?**

❏ A   Huntington's chorea
❏ B   Adult polycystic kidney disease
❏ C   Marfan's syndrome
❏ D   Haemochromatosis
❏ E   Neurofibromatosis

7.5 The substitution of the amino acid valine instead of the normal glutamic acid at position 6 of the β-globin chain is the genetic abnormality encountered in which one of the following types of congenital haemolytic anaemia?

❑ A Sickle cell anaemia
❑ B β-Thalassaemia
❑ C Hereditary spherocytosis
❑ D Glucose-6-phosphate dehydrogenase (G6PD) deficiency
❑ E Methaemoglobinaemia

7.6 Which one of the following inherited diseases is due to mutation in mitochondrial DNA?

❑ A Alport's syndrome
❑ B Leber's optic neuropathy
❑ C Noonan's syndrome
❑ D Fabry's disease
❑ E Marfan's syndrome

7.7 Which one of the following statements is true about haemochromatosis?

❑ A The primary defect is poor utilisation of iron by the bone marrow
❑ B Hypogonadism is due to haemosiderin deposition in the gonads
❑ C Hepatoma is a rare complication
❑ D Clinically significant renal parenchymal disease occurs in half of the cases
❑ E Diabetes mellitus is usually insulin dependent

7.8 Each of the following statements regarding X-linked recessive disorders is true EXCEPT?

❑ A A heterozygous female will transmit the trait to half of her daughters
❑ B All daughters born to an affected father and a normal mother will be carriers
❑ C Half of paternal uncles will be affected
❑ D Half the daughters of a heterozygous mother will be carriers
❑ E Heterozygous females occasionally exhibit mild features of the disease

8: HAEMATOLOGY

8.1 **Which one of the following findings is MOST useful in differentiating chronic myeloid leukaemia (CML) from a leukaemoid reaction?**

❏ A Philadelphia chromosome
❏ B Splenic enlargement
❏ C Low leucocyte alkaline phosphatase score
❏ D Hypercellular bone marrow
❏ E Elevated platelet count

8.2 **Which one of the following features is MOST suggestive of megaloblastic anaemia?**

❏ A Hypersegmented neutrophil in peripheral blood film
❏ B Atrophic gastritis
❏ C Pancytopenia
❏ D Low reticulocyte count
❏ E Raised LDH

8.3 **Which one of the following statements regarding iron deficiency anaemia is MOST accurate?**

❏ A It is commonly caused by dietary deficiency
❏ B Pins and needles in the hands and feet may indicate early peripheral neuropathy
❏ C Splenomegaly occurs in up to 50% of cases
❏ D Koilonychia is characteristic and rarely seen in other forms of anaemia
❏ E Reticulocyte count is often elevated

8.4 **Which one of the following features is MOST characteristic of Waldenström macroglobulinaemia?**

❏ A Bone pain
❏ B Monoclonal IgM peak
❏ C Renal impairment
❏ D Multiple osteolytic lesions
❏ E Absence of immune paresis

8.5 **Which one of the following features is MOST helpful in distinguishing β thalassaemia trait from iron deficiency anaemia (IDA)?**

- ❏ A Microcytosis
- ❏ B Haemoglobin A2 levels
- ❏ C Reduced haematocrit
- ❏ D Splenomegaly
- ❏ E Target cells on peripheral blood examination

8.6 **Which one of the following blood transfusion adverse effects is LEAST likely to be mediated by the donor WBC?**

- ❏ A Febrile non-haemolytic transfusion reactions (FNHTRs)
- ❏ B Transmission of AIDS
- ❏ C Transfusion related acute lung injury (TRALIs)
- ❏ D Alloimmunisation against platelets
- ❏ E Transmission of cytomegalovirus (CMV)

8.7 **Therapeutic plasmapheresis is considered MOST effective in which one of the following types of haemolytic anaemia?**

- ❏ A Haemolytic anaemia associated with *Mycoplasma pneumoniae*
- ❏ B Thalassaemia major
- ❏ C Systemic lupus erythematosus (SLE) associated haemolytic anaemia
- ❏ D Paroxysmal nocturnal haemoglobinuria (PNH)
- ❏ E Aplastic anaemia

8.8 **Plasma proteins that increase during the acute phase response include each of the following EXCEPT?**

- ❏ A Haptoglobin
- ❏ B Ceruloplasmin
- ❏ C Immunoglobulins
- ❏ D Fibrinogen
- ❏ E Ferritin

8.9 **Which one of the following clinical findings is NOT characteristic of chronic lymphatic leukaemia?**

☐ A Hypogammaglobulinaemia is often present at the time of the diagnosis

☐ B B-lymphocytes are the leukaemia cell line in the majority of cases

☐ C Bone marrow examination is essential to confirm the diagnosis

☐ D Coombs' test is positive in 10–20% of cases

☐ E It converts to lymphoma

8.10 **Which one of the following features is characteristic of immune thrombocytopenic purpura (ITP)?**

☐ A Infants born to a woman with ITP often presents with bleeding diathesis in the first 48 hours

☐ B Pancytopenia is a recognised complication

☐ C Leukaemic transformation occurs late in the disease

☐ D Splenomegaly is found in 50% of cases

☐ E Autoimmune haemolytic anaemia is a recognised association

8.11 **Which one of the following is NOT an accurate statement regarding hairy cell leukaemia?**

☐ A Female:male ratio of 10:2

☐ B Pancytopenia and splenomegaly are the usual presenting features

☐ C 'Dry tap' marrow aspirate despite the presence of marrow hypercellularity

☐ D Tartrate-resistant acid phosphatase (TRAP) stain is positive

☐ E Vasculitic skin lesions occur in one-third of cases

8.12 **In a patient with acute lymphoblastic leukaemia good prognostic signs include each of the following EXCEPT?**

☐ A Low initial leucocytes count

☐ B Age < 15 years

☐ C Mediastinal lymphadenopathy

☐ D Pre-B phenotype

☐ E cALLA type

8.13   Hyposplenism is rarely encountered in which one of the following conditions?

❏   A   Sickle cell disease
❏   B   Coeliac disease
❏   C   Systemic lupus erythematosus
❏   D   Myxoedema
❏   E   Dermatitis herpetiformis

8.14   Which one of the following is LEAST characteristic of idiopathic myelofibrosis?

❏   A   Leucoerythroblastic picture
❏   B   Extensive bone marrow sclerosis
❏   C   Splenomegaly
❏   D   Tear drop shaped red blood cells
❏   E   Terminal conversion to multiple myeloma

8.15   Which one of the following statements BEST describes haemophilia A?

❏   A   Petechiae are more common than soft tissue bleeding
❏   B   Bleeding time is prolonged
❏   C   Factor 8 inhibitors occur in 10% of patients receiving multiple factor 8 transfusion
❏   D   Iron deficiency anaemia is a frequent and persistent problem
❏   E   Joint deformity is rare despite the fact that haemarthrosis is one of the main recurrent manifestations

8.16   Thrombocytosis would occur in each of the following conditions EXCEPT?

❏   A   Ulcerative colitis
❏   B   Haemolytic-uraemic syndrome
❏   C   Polycythaemia rubra vera
❏   D   Iron deficiency anaemia
❏   E   Sickle cell disease

8.17   **Which one of the following is the MOST common cause of aplastic crisis in a patient with sickle cell disease?**

❏   A   Dehydration
❏   B   Respiratory syncytial virus infection
❏   C   Human parvovirus B19 infection
❏   D   Repeated blood transfusion
❏   E   *Haemophilus influenzae* septicaemia

8.18   **Compared with unfractionated heparin, low-molecular-weight (LMW) heparins have all the following advantages EXCEPT?**

❏   A   They do not bind antithrombin
❏   B   Their use is associated with low risk for heparin induced thrombocytopenia
❏   C   They have a longer half-life, allowing daily or twice-daily dosing
❏   D   Have low risk for bleeding
❏   E   They are produced by depolymerisation of unfractionated heparins

8.19   **Which one of the following conditions is LEAST associated with aplastic anaemia?**

❏   A   Paroxysmal nocturnal haemoglobinuria
❏   B   Pneumococcal pneumonia
❏   C   Parvovirus infection
❏   D   Thymoma
❏   E   Chloramphenicol therapy

8.20   **In transfusion haemosiderosis which one of the following statements is true?**

❏   A   Symptoms of iron overload usually develop when a total of 10 units of packed erythrocytes are transfused.
❏   B   Conduction defect is a frequent early symptom of cardiac involvement
❏   C   Diagnosis is readily made by assessment of serum ferritin level and liver biopsy
❏   D   D-penicillamine orally as a chelating agent is the treatment of choice
❏   E   Because of the associated chronic anaemia, patients with thalassaemia are very resistant to this disorder

8.21 **Which one of the following tumours is LEAST likely to present with pyrexia of undetermined origin?**

❏ A Hodgkin's lymphoma
❏ B Preleukaemia
❏ C Bronchial carcinoma
❏ D Atrial myxoma
❏ E Hypernephroma

8.22 **Which one of the following bone sites is the MOST common site involved in bone metastases from carcinomata?**

❏ A Ribs
❏ B Pelvis
❏ C Spine
❏ D Skull
❏ E Long bones

8.23 **Which one of the following statements is true about folic acid deficiency?**

❏ A Because of the high folate body stores, it will take more than two years for megaloblastic anaemia to develop after complete cessation of folic acid intake
❏ B Methotrexate induced folic acid deficiency is corrected by concomitant folic acid therapy
❏ C Intestinal bacterial overgrowth is regarded as one of the common causes
❏ D Causes abnormal neurological findings indistinguishable from that associated with B_{12} deficiency
❏ E Responsible for neural tube defect in the fetus

9: INFECTIOUS DISEASES

9.1 **Each of the following infections/disorders are associated with the genus *Chlamydia* EXCEPT?**

❏ A Q fever
❏ B Lymphogranuloma venereum (LGV)
❏ C Psittacosis ornithosis
❏ D Trachoma
❏ E Reiter's syndrome

9.2 **Which one of the following is LEAST characteristic of haemolytic uraemic syndrome (HUS)?**

❏ A More common in children
❏ B Fragmented red blood cells on peripheral blood film examination
❏ C Fever and transient cerebral disorders are frequently present
❏ D *E. coli* is rarely isolated from the blood
❏ E Complete recovery is expected in most cases

9.3 **Which one of the following statements is NOT accurate regarding malaria?**

❏ A In *P. vivax* fever and rigors usually manifest two weeks after an infected mosquito bite
❏ B In *P. malariae* a relapse can occur even two years after the patient has left an area prone to malaria
❏ C Chloroquine is ineffective in the treatment of *P. falciparum* infection
❏ D Sickle cell trait protects against malaria
❏ E Blood film smear examination is usually diagnostic

9.4   A 60-year-old woman is convalescing in hospital following total right knee replacement surgery undertaken three weeks ago. She develops headache, chills and a fever of 39.2°C. On examination the right knee is red, hot and very tender. Synovial fluid aspirate reports the growth of Gram-positive cocci. Which one of the following is the MOST likely organism?

- ❏ A *Staphylococcus epidermidis*
- ❏ B *Pseudomona aeruginosa*
- ❏ C *Streptococcus pneumoniae*
- ❏ D *Staphylococcus aureus*
- ❏ E *Haemophilus influenzae*

9.5   Arthropod-borne diseases include each of the following EXCEPT?

- ❏ A Malaria
- ❏ B Hydatid cyst
- ❏ C Trypanosomiasis
- ❏ D Leishmaniasis
- ❏ E Lyme disease

9.6   In multiple drug resistant tuberculosis (MDR-TB) which one of the following statements is NOT accurate?

- ❏ A Usually caused by *Mycobacterium avium-intracellulare* (MAI)
- ❏ B AIDS has increased the incidence of MDR-TB
- ❏ C Sputum smear for acid-fast bacilli is often positive
- ❏ D Directly observed therapy or supervised therapy is recommended
- ❏ E Quinolones such as ciproxin have an anti-TB effect

9.7   A 54-year-old woman presents to her doctor with a painful rash that she first noticed the day before. On examination, a group of erythematous vesicles is noted over the right flank in the T10 dermatome distribution. Reasonable treatment options at this time include all of the following EXCEPT?

- ❏ A Famciclovir
- ❏ B Acyclovir
- ❏ C Steroids
- ❏ D Carbamazepine
- ❏ E Morphine

9.8 A 21-year-old student taking the oral contraceptive pill develops pain and soreness around the genitals. She has just completed an elective year in the USA. On examination there are multiple, shallow and tender ulcers at the skin and mucous membrane of the vagina. The most probable diagnosis is?

- ❏ A Genital herpes
- ❏ B Chancroid
- ❏ C Granuloma inguinale
- ❏ D Primary syphilis
- ❏ E Lymphogranuloma venereum

9.9 A 19-year-old female university student presents with fever and headache. On examination she is conscious but has neck stiffness. The cerebrospinal fluid Gram stain shows intracellular Gram-negative diplococci. The most probable diagnosis is?

- ❏ A Meningococcal meningitis
- ❏ B *Haemophilus influenzae* meningitis
- ❏ C *Streptococcus pneumonia* meningitis
- ❏ D *Listeria* monocytogenes
- ❏ E *E. coli* meningitis

9.10 A 70-year-old man known to have NIDDM was admitted with pain and swelling in the left ear and face. On examination the external ear is red, tender and swollen. There is a small amount of purulent discharge from the external auditory canal with crust covering the skin. The left side of the face is swollen, with tenderness over the left temporal bone. The primary micro-organism most probably responsible for this infection is?

- ❏ A *Pseudomonas aeruginosa*
- ❏ B *Staphylococcus aureus*
- ❏ C *Streptococcus pneumoniae*
- ❏ D *Listeria monocytogenes*
- ❏ E *Haemophilus influenzae*

9.11   Which one of the following statements is true with regard to Legionnaires' disease?

❑   A   *Legionella pneumophila* is a Gram-positive rod
❑   B   The urinary antigen test for *Legionella* species has low sensitivity and is not particularly specific
❑   C   The infection is generally confined to immunocompromised patients
❑   D   The beta-lactam group of drugs are now regarded as the drug of choice against *Legionella* species
❑   E   Hyponatraemia occurs significantly more often in Legionnaires' disease than in other pneumonias

9.12   Which one of the following is NOT true regarding indium leucocyte study (^{111}In-labelled leucocyte)?

❑   A   The entire body can be checked for infectious disease sites
❑   B   Specifically used to detect splenic abscess
❑   C   Very useful in evaluating the activity of IBD
❑   D   False-negative results might be obtained in leucopenic patient
❑   E   False-positive diagnosis of an abscess of the abdomen may be the result of swallowing purulent sputum

9.13   Which one of the following statements with regard to Kaposi's sarcoma (KS) is true?

❑   A   The incidence of KS in AIDS has been in progressive decline since the early 90s
❑   B   There is a 400 times increased risk of KS among patients with congenital immune deficiency
❑   C   Respiratory tract disease is regarded as the most common initial manifestation
❑   D   In recent years the incidence of KS in AIDS in heterosexual men has exceeded that in homosexual and bisexual men
❑   E   KS is rarely encountered in organ transplant patients

9.14 **Each of the following is true regarding AIDS EXCEPT?**

❑ A Oral hairy leukoplakia is probably caused by Epstein-Barr virus (EBV)

❑ B Lymph node biopsy and a blood culture that grew *Mycobacterium avium-intracellulare* would confirm that HIV is the cause of the generalised lymphadenopathy

❑ C Sputum culture is likely to provide diagnostic results for *Pneumocystis carinii*

❑ D CMV infection is the most common cause of retinitis in AIDS

❑ E Kaposi's sarcoma is almost never recognised among AIDS patients who are not homosexual or bisexual

9.15 **There are some important differences between the life-cycles of *Plasmodium vivax* and that of *Plasmodium falciparum*. From the list below, which one life-cycle stage occurs with *P. vivax* but not with *P. falciparum* infection?**

❑ A Gametocytes

❑ B Hypnozoites

❑ C Schizonts

❑ D Sporozoites

❑ E Trophozoites

9.16 **An 5-year-old boy is admitted with a temperature of 39.6°C and a rash consisting of numerous dusky pink macules and papules. He became unwell 6 days ago, when his mother noticed that he had a dry cough, red eyes and a temperature. The rash started 2 days prior to admission, appearing on his face initially, but then spreading to the trunk and limbs. He was in contact with a boy with a similar rash 10 days ago. There is no significant past medical history. He had not received all his childhood immunisations due to parental concerns regarding vaccine safety. Which one of the following is the likely cause of his rash?**

❑ A Epstein-Barr virus

❑ B Measles virus

❑ C Parvovirus B19

❑ D Rubella virus

❑ E Mumps virus

9.17   You have been informed that an organism is growing in both the aerobic and the anaerobic blood-culture bottles that you obtained from a patient yesterday. A Gram-positive coccus has been isolated, which is growing in small clusters. On further laboratory testing, it is shown to cause the coagulation of fibrinogen to a fibrin clot when added to diluted plasma in a test-tube. What is the most likely organism?

❏   A   *Enterobacter cloacae*
❏   B   *Staphylococcus aureus*
❏   C   *Staphylococcus epidermidis*
❏   D   *Streptococcus pneumoniae*
❏   E   *Streptococcus pyogenes*

9.18   A 44-year-old woman who is taking oral prednisolone for a flare-up of her rheumatoid arthritis is planning a 6-week holiday to a remote jungle region of Latin America. She has completed her childhood vaccination programme, and received a polio booster 8 years ago. However, she has heard that she requires further travel vaccinations. Her travel agent has suggested the items below, but she is a bit concerned about the safety of these given her medical history. Which one of the following vaccines do you feel poses the greatest difficulty?

❏   A   Polio
❏   B   Hepatitis A
❏   C   Tetanus
❏   D   Typhoid Vi
❏   E   Yellow fever

9.19   A 49-year-old woman is referred to you by her GP for suspected chronic fatigue syndrome. Which one of the following features would suggest that this was an incorrect diagnosis ?

❏   A   Dysphagia
❏   B   Frequent headaches
❏   C   Memory impairment
❏   D   Recurrent sore throats
❏   E   Severe myalgia

9.20   A 52-year-old man wishes to commence therapy for chronic hepatitis C virus (HCV) infection. He wishes to take a regime which has the best chance of conferring sustained virological success. Which one of the following treatment options would you recommend ?

- ❏   A   α interferon alone
- ❏   B   α interferon with ribavirin
- ❏   C   Ribavirin alone
- ❏   D   Ribavirin with lamivudine
- ❏   E   Lamivudine alone

10: NEPHROLOGY

10.1   Which one of the following types of glomerulonephritis is LEAST likely to be associated with low complement levels?

- ❑ A   Post-streptococcal glomerulonephritis
- ❑ B   Diffuse proliferative glomerulonephritis associated with systemic lupus erythematosus
- ❑ C   Subacute bacterial endocarditis
- ❑ D   Primary membranous glomerulonephritis
- ❑ E   Primary type 1 membranoproliferative glomerulonephritis

10.2   Which one of the following statements BEST describes the hepatorenal syndrome?

- ❑ A   It is due to glomerulonephritis associated liver disease
- ❑ B   Almost all patients have ascites and are usually jaundiced
- ❑ C   Marked proteinuria is the hallmark of the disease
- ❑ D   *E. coli* are often isolated on blood culture
- ❑ E   Complete recovery is expected in the majority of cases

10.3   The presence of which one of the following features is MOST helpful in distinguishing chronic from acute renal failure?

- ❑ A   Seizures
- ❑ B   Bilateral small kidneys
- ❑ C   Hypocalcaemia
- ❑ D   Dilute urine with high urine sodium
- ❑ E   Acute pulmonary oedema

10.4   Which one of the following vasculitides is more often associated with renal involvement?

- ❑ A   Churg-Strauss syndrome
- ❑ B   Takayasu's arteritis
- ❑ C   Microscopic polyangiitis
- ❑ D   Cryoglobulinaemic vasculitis
- ❑ E   Henoch-Schönlein purpura

10.5   **Which one of the following is LEAST suggestive of Goodpasture's syndrome?**

❏   A   Autosomal recessive inheritance
❏   B   More common in young males
❏   C   Linear deposit at the glomerular basement membrane on indirect immunofluorescent test
❏   D   Pulmonary haemorrhage usually precedes renal involvement
❏   E   Vasculitic skin rash is often encountered early in the disease

10.6   **Which one of the following statements is true regarding retroperitoneal fibrosis?**

❏   A   Low back pain is the most common presenting symptom
❏   B   Bilateral swelling of the legs is often due to inferior vena-caval obstruction
❏   C   Pizotifen (migraine treatment) is implicated in causing similar disease
❏   D   Renal failure is due to fibrous tissue infiltrating the kidneys
❏   E   Hashimoto's thyroiditis is a recognised association

10.7   **Which one of the following features is characteristic of Bartter's syndrome?**

❏   A   Hypokalaemia with hypertension
❏   B   Reduced urinary excretion of potassium and chloride
❏   C   Good response to ACE inhibitors
❏   D   Low renin and aldosterone
❏   E   Hyperplasia of the juxtaglomerular apparatus

10.8   **Which one of the following conditions is MOST commonly associated with large kidneys despite advanced renal failure?**

❏   A   Amyloidosis
❏   B   Hypertensive nephrosclerosis
❏   C   Membranous glomerulonephritis
❏   D   Systemic sclerosis
❏   E   Analgesic nephropathy

10.9 A 10-year-old boy is hospitalised because of a recent melaena and fever (38°C). The patient also complains of arthralgia involving the knees and the ankles. On examination he has a purpuric rash involving the legs. Urinalysis discloses proteinuria with microscopic haematuria. A biopsy of the purpuric lesion reveals leucocytoclastic vasculitis in the small vessels. Which one of the following statements is true about this boy's illness?

❑ A The purpuric skin rash is due to associated thrombocytopenia
❑ B Active urinary sediment with RBC casts indicates glomerulonephritis
❑ C Identification of anti-glomerular basement membrane antibodies is expected in half of the cases
❑ D pANCA is positive in two-thirds of the cases
❑ E Renal granulomas are pathognomonic for this disorder

10.10 Which one of the following systemic disorders is LEAST associated with glomerulonephritis?

❑ A Malaria
❑ B Goodpasture's disease
❑ C Sarcoidosis
❑ D Wegener's granulomatosis
❑ E Henoch-Schönlein purpura

10.11 Crystal-induced acute renal failure can be caused by each of the following EXCEPT?

❑ A Allopurinol
❑ B Sulphonamide antibiotics
❑ C Acyclovir
❑ D Ethylene glycol
❑ E Vitamin C

10.12 Each of the following statements is true regarding general urine examination EXCEPT?

❏ A   Hyaline casts are seen in a normal individual
❏ B   Green urine colour may be due to urinary tract infection (UTI) caused by *Pseudomonas aeruginosa*
❏ C   Granular casts indicate renal parenchymal disease
❏ D   Dysmorphic red blood cells indicate glomerular disease
❏ E   Fat globules on hyaline cast are often encountered in pyelonephritis

10.13 A 45-year-old man is admitted with acute renal failure of undetermined aetiology. His creatinine is 1564 μmol/l and his urea is 76 mmol/l. His blood pressure is 200/110 mmHg, he is oliguric, and he has pulmonary oedema confirmed on chest radiography. A dual lumen dialysis line is inserted into his right subclavian vein, and the position confirmed by chest radiograph. He is urgently commenced on haemodialysis, in a recumbent position, with a target weight loss of 1.5kg. One hour into dialysis, he begins to complain of nausea, headache, and blurred vision. Shortly afterwards, he becomes confused and disorientated. His blood pressure is 180/100 mmHg. Which one of the following is the MOST likely explanation?

❏ A   Air embolism
❏ B   Reaction to hypotonic dialysate
❏ C   Dysequilibrium syndrome
❏ D   Pericardial tamponade
❏ E   Intravascular volume contraction resulting from rapid ultrafiltration

10.14 Which one of the following drug interactions is false?

❏ A   Cyclosporin A and simvastatin causing rhabdomyolysis
❏ B   Mycophenolate mofetil and nifedipine causing tinnitus
❏ C   Azathioprine and allopurinol causing bone marrow suppression
❏ D   Tacrolimus potentiated by erythromycin
❏ E   Prednisolone antagonising frusemide

10.15   **Wilms' tumour is most strongly associated with which one of the following aetiological factors?**

❑   A   Cadmium exposure
❑   B   Smoking
❑   C   Naphthylamine
❑   D   Deletion on short arm of chromosome 11
❑   E   Balkan nephropathy

10.16   **Which one of the following features would NOT be suggestive of a renal aetiology in a hypertensive patient?**

❑   A   Red nodules on the face and mental retardation
❑   B   Wheezing, flushing and diarrhoea
❑   C   Nerve deafness
❑   D   Asymmetrical pulses
❑   E   Multiple café au lait spots and subcutaneous nodules

10.17   **Which one of the following is a risk factor for poor prognosis in a patient with acute Wegener's disease?**

❑   A   Female sex
❑   B   cANCA positivity
❑   C   100% active crescents on renal biopsy
❑   D   Extrarenal vasculitis
❑   E   Renal involvement

10.18   **Which one of the following, when seen in a pregnant woman, is not likely to be physiological?**

❑   A   Glycosuria
❑   B   Haematuria
❑   C   Ketonuria
❑   D   Plasma osmolality 277mOsmol/kg
❑   E   Ureteral dilatation

10: Nephrology

11: NEUROLOGY

11.1 In a patient with diplopia which one of the following findings is MOST suggestive of myasthenia gravis?

- ❏ A Symmetrical external ocular muscle weakness
- ❏ B Preserved pupillary light reflex with absent accommodation reflex
- ❏ C Thymoma on computed tomography scan (CT scan) of the chest
- ❏ D Elevated creatinine phosphokinase (CPK)
- ❏ E Proptosis

11.2 Which one of the following features is MOST typical of cavernous sinus thrombosis?

- ❏ A Double vision on looking upward
- ❏ B Papilloedema is an early feature
- ❏ C Ipsilateral lower motor facial nerve palsy
- ❏ D Loss of pin prick sensation around the chin area
- ❏ E Difficulty in swallowing

11.3 Which one of the following statements is MOST accurate about chronic subdural haematoma?

- ❏ A The trauma to the head is usually minor and often forgotten by the patient
- ❏ B Neck stiffness is an early feature
- ❏ C Headache is often absent
- ❏ D Lumbar puncture and CSF analysis should be done immediately on patient arrival
- ❏ E Injury to the middle meningeal artery is the usual cause of the haematoma

11.4 Which one of the following structures within the central nervous system (CNS) is LEAST pain sensitive?

- ❏ A Pia mater
- ❏ B Dura mater
- ❏ C Cranial nerve X
- ❏ D Parietal lobe veins
- ❏ E Middle cerebral artery

11.5 **Which one of the following neurological findings is MOST helpful in differentiating subacute combined degeneration of the cord from multiple sclerosis?**

❑ A Bilateral Babinski's sign
❑ B Absent ankle jerk
❑ C Optic atrophy
❑ D 'Barber's chair' sign
❑ E Ataxia

11.6 **Which one of the following is MOST suggestive of essential tremor?**

❑ A Often associated with cogwheel rigidity
❑ B Improves with intentional movement
❑ C Made worse with alcohol
❑ D Strong familial tendency
❑ E Tends to improve with age

11.7 **Which one of the following is MOST suggestive of a lesion of the sciatic nerve?**

❑ A Absent knee tendon jerk
❑ B Foot drop
❑ C Inability to flex the hip
❑ D Decreased sensation on anterior thigh and medial leg
❑ E Intervertebral disc prolapse at L2/L3 levels

11.8 **Which one of the following pathological abnormalities is characteristically found in patients with Parkinson's disease?**

❑ A Mallory bodies
❑ B Lewy bodies
❑ C Neurofibrillary tangles
❑ D Pick bodies
❑ E Negri bodies

11.9 **Chorea is a recognised feature of each of the following disorders EXCEPT?**

❏ A Wilson's disease
❏ B Haemochromatosis
❏ C Long term use of the oral contraceptive pill
❏ D Lupus erythematosus
❏ E Polycythaemia rubra vera

11.10 **Autonomic neuropathy is rarely encountered in which one of the following conditions?**

❏ A Shy-Drager syndrome
❏ B Guillain-Barré syndrome
❏ C Amyloidosis
❏ D Chronic alcoholism
❏ E Myasthenia gravis

11.11 **A 32-year-old woman is referred with a two-week history of blurred vision, unsteady gait and numbness in the right hand. She has experienced similar short lived attacks in the past. One year ago, she abruptly lost function in the left hand which returned to normal after five days. On examination she has bilateral horizontal nystagmus and generalised hyperreflexia. There is reduced vibration sense in the limbs and central scotoma. The brain MRI scan showed multiple lesions in the white matter with no surrounding oedema at the periventricular area and cerebellum. The MOST probable diagnosis is?**

❏ A Thrombophilia with multiple cerebral infarct
❏ B Syringomyelia
❏ C Metastatic tumour to brain
❏ D Multiple sclerosis
❏ E Amyotrophic lateral sclerosis

11.12 **Which one of the following statements concerning syringomyelia/syringobulbia is NOT accurate?**

❏ A Frequently associated with congenital craniocervical malformations

❏ B Loss of pain and position sense with preservation of touch and temperature

❏ C Bilateral Babinski reflex

❏ D Dysphonia and tongue atrophy

❏ E Nystagmus

11.13 **A 40-year-old banker came to the emergency room complaining of intense headache of two hours duration. The pain is localised around the right eye and is associated with tearing and redness of the eye. The patient reported he has had similar episodes over the last year. He also admits that these episodes occurred every day for a few weeks with one to three attacks a day which last for one to two hours, frequently at night. After six weeks, the attacks stopped. He lost his job six months ago and has noticed an increase in the intensity of the pain since. Examination reveals drooping of the eyelid and small pupil on the right side. Which one of the following is the MOST probable diagnosis?**

❏ A Migraine

❏ B Tension-type headache

❏ C Iritis associated headache

❏ D Cerebral tumour

❏ E Cluster headache

11.14 A 70-year-old-man arrives at the accident and emergency department an hour after he felt light headed and collapsed to the ground. He told the two paramedics who accompanied him that he has double vision whenever he looks to the right. On examination he is conscious and alert. There is diplopia, ptosis and dilated pupil on the left. He also has right hemiplegia. Occlusion of which one of the following arteries is responsible for the above neurological deficit in this patient?

- ❏ A Branch of the basilar artery
- ❏ B Posterior cerebral artery
- ❏ C Anterior cerebral artery
- ❏ D Middle cerebral artery
- ❏ E Vertebral artery

11.15 A 33-year-old-female teacher presents with sudden onset of weakness, numbness and paraesthesia in the right leg. She has light headedness and an electric shock like feeling from the neck down the spine whenever she bends her head forward. She denies any history of fits but her brother who is sixteen years old suffers with epilepsy. On examination there is evidence of profound weakness and reduced pin prick sensation in the right leg. Horizontal nystagmus on looking to the right is evident. The most appropriate test at this stage is?

- ❏ A Nerve conduction study (NCS)
- ❏ B Visual evoked potentials (VEPs)
- ❏ C Electromyography (EMG)
- ❏ D Polysomnography
- ❏ E Electroencephalograph (EEG)

11.16 In multiple sclerosis each of the following is true EXCEPT?

- ❏ A Symptoms worsen with elevation of body temperature
- ❏ B Pregnancy has no ill effect on the course of the disease
- ❏ C Bilateral facial nerve palsy occurs in 50% of cases
- ❏ D Predominant sensory symptoms at presentation carry better prognosis
- ❏ E Interferon-alpha reduces the relapse frequency in selected case

11.17 **Human prion disease comprises each of the following disorders EXCEPT?**

❏ A Kuru
❏ B Creutzfeldt-Jakob disease
❏ C Gerstmann Sträussler disease
❏ D Fatal familial insomnia
❏ E Progressive multifocal leucoencephalopathy

11.18 **Elevated cerebrospinal fluid gamma globulin concentration has been described in each of the following conditions EXCEPT?**

❏ A Myasthenia gravis
❏ B Subacute sclerosing panencephalitis
❏ C Cerebral lupus
❏ D Multiple sclerosis
❏ E Guillain-Barré syndrome

11.19 **Which one of the following is NOT true regarding primary empty sella syndrome?**

❏ A The pituitary gland is congenitally absent
❏ B Cerebrospinal fluid rhinorrhoea is a recognised presenting feature
❏ C More common in multiparous obese women
❏ D Associated with systemic hypertension
❏ E Complete pituitary evaluation may reveal low TSH

11.20 **With regard to benign intracranial hypertension (BIH) each of the following is true EXCEPT?**

❏ A Loss of vision is the only serious complication
❏ B Papilloedema is almost always present
❏ C The CSF pressure recording is within normal limit in 50% of cases
❏ D Long term steroid therapy is a possible aetiological factor
❏ E Diplopia when manifest is usually a false localizing sign

12: OPHTHALMOLOGY

12.1 Which one of the following is LEAST helpful in differentiating optic neuritis from papilloedema?

❏ A Pain behind the eye on presentation
❏ B Swelling of the optic disc on ophthalmoscopic examination of the retina
❏ C Central scotoma
❏ D Reduced visual acuity
❏ E History of recurrent transient arm weakness

12.2 Altitudinal hemianopia is a cardinal feature in a patient who

❏ A Denies the fact he is blind
❏ B Is 72 years old with macular degeneration
❏ C Is 70 years old with headache, vomiting and swelling of the optic disc
❏ D Is a 74-year-old man with multiple cholesterol emboli on fundoscopy
❏ E Has coarse facial features, large lips and spade like fingers

12.3 A sixty-year-old man presents with a week's history of painless diplopia first noticed when reading. The images are constantly horizontally and vertically separated, although he comments that the degree of separation varies. On examination the visual acuities are 6/6 in either eye. There is no pupil abnormality. There is a left ptosis, partially covering the pupil and reduced abduction and depression of the left eye, both in abduction and adduction, with other ocular movements appearing normal. There is no other abnormality on examination. Which one of the following is the MOST likely diagnosis?

❏ A Orbital apex syndrome
❏ B Sixth nerve palsy
❏ C Third nerve palsy
❏ D Fourth nerve palsy
❏ E Ocular myaesthenia gravis

12.4 **A 22-year-old man with ulcerative colitis and chronic lower back pain complains of a red painful eye. Which one of the following is likely to be present on examination?**

❏ A Purulent discharge
❏ B Photophobia on ophthalmoscopy
❏ C A dilated pupil
❏ D Profound visual loss
❏ E Retinal haemorrhages

13: PSYCHIATRY

13.1 Which one of the following features is MOST helpful in distinguishing dementia from severe depression?

- ❑ A Persistent headache
- ❑ B Weight loss
- ❑ C Poor attention spans
- ❑ D Grasp reflex
- ❑ E Social withdrawal

13.2 The risk of suicide is higher in which one of the following individuals?

- ❑ A A 45-year-old woman with a history of suicide attempts
- ❑ B A married man with two children
- ❑ C A 50-year-old man with prior suicide attempts
- ❑ D A 30-year-old man recently diagnosed with a positive HIV test
- ❑ E A 25-year-old woman with a history of drug overdose

13.3 Which one of the following statements is accurate about obsessive-compulsive disorders (OCD)?

- ❑ A Feeling of guilt is the core abnormal behaviour that drives the compulsions
- ❑ B Thought insertion and compulsive acts are the essential features
- ❑ C The patient gets pleasure from the experience
- ❑ D The disorder may be a sequel of group A β-haemolytic streptococcal pharyngitis
- ❑ E Major tranquillizers are the mainstay of treatment

13.4 A 28-year-old-female is admitted with recurrent epileptic fits. She is known to have epilepsy and has been taking phenytoin for five years, but her fits are not controlled. During her stay the resident doctor was able to make the patient respond to verbal commands during the fit and he thought that the fits he witnessed were probably psychogenic non-epileptic seizures (pseudoseizures). In this patient the presence of which one of the following features would be MOST helpful in establishing the diagnosis of genuine epileptic fits?

- ❏ A Urinary incontinence
- ❏ B Tongue biting
- ❏ C Pelvic thrusting
- ❏ D History of two previous admissions with status epilepticus
- ❏ E Family history of epilepsy (sister)

13.5 An 18-year-old man is seen in outpatients with his mother who complains that he is slow off the mark, has problems interacting with others and has difficulty concentrating. When you examine him you discover a high arched palate, mitral valve prolapse, joint laxity, strabismus and large ears. Which one of the following investigations would be MOST useful in reaching a diagnosis?

- ❏ A Chromosomal analysis
- ❏ B Karyotyping
- ❏ C CT scan of his head
- ❏ D Urinary homocystine
- ❏ E Urinary excretion of hydroxyproline

13.6 Which one of the following statements best fits with a diagnosis of tardive dyskinesia?

- ❏ A Fixed contortions of the muscles of the head, neck and upper limbs
- ❏ B Occurring within a few days of administration of an antipsychotic
- ❏ C Abnormal involuntary movements, typically choreoathetoid and usually complex, rapid and stereotyped
- ❏ D Muscular rigidity, tremor and bradykinesia
- ❏ E It is always reversible

13.7 **Which one of the following is NOT considered to be an organic brain syndrome?**

- ❏ A Dementia in Pick's disease
- ❏ B Multi-infarct dementia
- ❏ C Delirium
- ❏ D Post concussional syndrome
- ❏ E Ganser's syndrome

13.8 **A man of 50 years presents following the death of his wife, which one of the following is going to heighten your suspicion of an abnormal grief reaction?**

- ❏ A A brief episode of seeing the dead person
- ❏ B Poor concentration
- ❏ C Poor memory
- ❏ D Delayed or absent grief
- ❏ E Searching for the deceased

13.9 **A 45-year-old man with a history of paranoid schizophrenia is brought to casualty by the police as he has been 'behaving bizarrely'. There are no psychiatric beds available and he is admitted to the medical short stay unit with continual monitoring from a psychiatric nurse. After a night's sleep he appeared settled and co-operative but the next day he became extremely agitated. He screams that he can see 'people crawling all over the walls'. He looks terrified and highly distractible and gazes intermittently at the walls. At times he appears drowsy and at others hyper-alert. He is disoriented in time and place but not person. A full physical examination was impossible but he looks tremulous and is sweating profusely and staggers across the cubicle with an ataxic gait. Which one of the following is the MOST likely diagnosis?**

- ❏ A Exacerbation of his psychotic illness
- ❏ B Delirium due to drug withdrawal
- ❏ C Drug induced psychosis
- ❏ D Head injury
- ❏ E Neuroleptic malignant syndrome

13.10 A 34-year-old presents to casualty complaining that he has had an electrical chip inserted in his head which is giving him 'great power' and sending him 'messages that I am the one'. He also claims that his legs are 'moved by the great force.' These experiences began about 9 months ago but only became troubling in the past few days. He appears slightly perplexed and concerned. However he is settled and sits quietly in casualty while awaiting further assessment. Which one of the following is the MOST likely underlying diagnosis?

❏ A Bipolar affective disorder
❏ B Paranoid schizophrenia
❏ C Drug induced psychosis
❏ D Cotard's syndrome
❏ E Organic psychotic disorder

13.11 A 70-year-old man is brought to outpatient clinic by his son. The son complains that his father's personality has changed completely over the past year. Even at best he is forgetful and 'switched off', at worst he is drowsy and unresponsive. He is particularly concerned that his father has claimed to 'see things that aren't really there'. Over the past few weeks he has also been tripping a lot on the carpet and is no longer safe on the stairs going to his bedroom unaccompanied. The GP gave the patient a small dose of a neuroleptic which 'made things a million times worse'. On examination he has an inexpressive face, with a mild resting tremor and some axial rigidity. There is no other focal neurology. On mini mental state examination he scores 20/30. Which one of the following is the MOST likely primary brain pathology?

❏ A Neurofibrillary tangles
❏ B Normal brain
❏ C Multiple infarct in the grey matter
❏ D Lewy bodies
❏ E Pick bodies

13.12 A 25-year-old man is started on chlorpromazine having been
diagnosed as suffering from paranoid schizophrenia. Two
months later he is seen in clinic as an emergency due to
concerns from his friends over an apparent deterioration in his
mental state. The patient complains of an extremely distressing
sense of restlessness and a complete inability to remain still.
On examination he shifts constantly in his chair and fidgets
with his coat. There is a slight increase in tone on the right side
and a detectable resting tremor in the hands. He describes
some vague feelings of 'being watched' but there are no other
psychotic symptoms elicited. Which one of the following is the
MOST likely diagnosis?

- ❏ A Acute dystonic reaction due to chlorpromazine
- ❏ B Breakthrough of his psychotic symptoms
- ❏ C Akathisia
- ❏ D Tardive dyskinesia
- ❏ E Tardive dystonia

13: Psychiatry

14: RESPIRATORY MEDICINE

14.1 **In a cyanosed patient which one of the following statements is accurate?**

❏ A The PaO_2 at its best is not > 50 mmHg (7 kpascal)
❏ B In methaemoglobinaemia the PaO_2 is never above 50 mmHg (7 kpascal)
❏ C The expected reduced haemoglobin level is around 3 g/l
❏ D The blue tinge of the skin and mucous membrane is due to CO_2 retention
❏ E O_2 therapy should be avoided as it may worsen hypercapnia

14.2 **Which one of the following clinical findings is MOST suggestive of pulmonary embolism (PE)?**

❏ A Spiking temperature of 39°C lasting more than one week
❏ B Haemoptysis of more than 5 ml with negative chest X-ray
❏ C Chest pain worse on deep breathing and respiratory rate of 26/min
❏ D Recurrent chest pain in the same location
❏ E Chest pain on lying flat

14.3 **Which one of the following conditions is MOST likely to be associated with low FEV_1 and normal TLCO?**

❏ A Asthma
❏ B Emphysema
❏ C Sarcoidosis
❏ D Pulmonary hypertension
❏ E Fibrosing alveolitis

14.4 **Which one of the following features is rarely encountered in patients with sleep apnoea syndrome?**

❏ A Female gender
❏ B Day time sleepiness
❏ C Hypertension
❏ D Large neck size
❏ E Snoring

14.5 **Which one of the following features is MOST accurate regarding *Pneumocystis carinii* pneumonia (PCP)?**

❏ A Occurs exclusively in AIDS
❏ B Pleural effusion is frequently bilateral
❏ C Auscultation of the lungs usually reveals no abnormality
❏ D Blood culture is positive in one-third of cases
❏ E Metronidazole is the treatment of choice

14.6 **Which one of the following features is MOST characteristic of cystic fibrosis?**

❏ A Inherited as autosomal dominant
❏ B Pancreatic insufficiency is almost always identified in adult patients
❏ C In patients with recurrent chest infections *Pseudomonas cepacia* is the most frequent organism isolated from sputum
❏ D Family members who carry the gene are at risk of developing mild recurrent bronchitis
❏ E Patients typically have reduced levels of sodium and chloride in the sweat

14.7 **A 28-year-old black nurse develops painful nodules on the shin of both legs. She has low grade fever and has lost 5 kg in the two months prior to her presentation. Her chest X-ray shows bilateral hilar lymphadenopathy. The MOST likely outcome of this patient's illness is?**

❏ A Complete remission after appropriate course of steroid and cytotoxic drugs
❏ B Complete remission without any specific treatment
❏ C Complete initial remission soon interrupted by increasing relapses
❏ D Diffuse reticulo-nodular changes in the lung and progressive shortness of breath
❏ E Generalised lymphadenopathy and progressive wasting in 5–10 years

14.8   **Which one of the following features is MOST characteristic of small cell bronchial carcinoma?**

☐   A   History of prior asbestos exposure is usually obtained
☐   B   Hyponatraemia
☐   C   Known as small cell because the cancer cell origin is from small lymphocytes
☐   D   It has a relatively better prognosis when compared with other bronchial cancers
☐   E   Surgery is often the only defined treatment

14.9   **Exercise-induced asthma can be described by each of the following EXCEPT?**

☐   A   More common in children than in adults
☐   B   Worse in winter than in summer
☐   C   Grass pollens can induce bronchospasm
☐   D   Exacerbations are related to cooling of the airway
☐   E   Inhaled steroids bring acute attacks under control within 60–90 minutes

14.10   **Which one of the following conditions is rarely associated with pulmonary infiltrates and peripheral eosinophilia?**

☐   A   Allergic bronchopulmonary aspergillosis
☐   B   Löeffler's syndrome
☐   C   Churg-Strauss syndrome
☐   D   Sulphonamide therapy
☐   E   Fibrosing alveolitis

14.11   **Which one of the following statements with regard to sarcoidosis is true?**

☐   A   Parenchymal lung disease is often accompanied with pleural effusion
☐   B   Clubbing of the fingers is an early feature
☐   C   Jaundice and portal hypertension are the predominant features of hepatic sarcoidosis
☐   D   A positive tuberculin test in a patient with chronic sarcoidosis is suggestive of concomitant tuberculosis
☐   E   Hypercalcaemia when it manifests is usually resistant to steroid therapy

14.12   **Each of the following is true about ventilation perfusion (V/Q) scan of the lung EXCEPT?**

❏   A   Previous pulmonary embolism gives false positive results many years after the initial incident

❏   B   Excludes the diagnosis of pulmonary embolism when the result is normal

❏   C   The findings are more informative if the chest X-ray is normal

❏   D   The diagnosis of pulmonary embolism is of higher probability when there is single sub-segmental mismatch

❏   E   Pulmonary arterio-venous malformation gives false positive result

14.13   **A 21-year-old medical student presents with confusion and dyspnoea 24 hours after fracturing his left femur in a ski competition. Which one of the following skin lesions is expected on physical examination?**

❏   A   Multiple vesicular lesions on the upper back

❏   B   Target lesions on the chest

❏   C   Tender red nodules on the shin

❏   D   Multiple petechiae in both axillae

❏   E   Palpable purpura on the buttock

14.14   **Most cases of community acquired pneumonia are caused by which one of the following?**

❏   A   *Streptococcus pneumoniae*

❏   B   *Mycoplasma pneumoniae*

❏   C   *Staphylococcus aureus*

❏   D   *Haemophilus influenzae*

❏   E   Viral pneumonia

14.15 **Which one of the following statements is NOT true about dyspnoea?**

❏ A In diaphragmatic paralysis it occurs immediately after lying down

❏ B When it improves during exercise, psychogenic hyperventilation may be the cause

❏ C In asthma it occurs shortly after cessation of exercise

❏ D In pulmonary venous congestion it occurs immediately after sleep

❏ E In hypersensitivity pneumonitis is worse in late afternoon and improves over the weekend

14.16 **A 30-year-old male presents with a cough and expectoration of greenish sputum. He is known to have had recurrent chest infections with progressive shortness of breath since early childhood. A high resolution CT scan of the chest shows dilated airways in both lower lobes and in the lingula. When seen in cross section, the dilated airways have a ring-like appearance. One of his brothers had a similar problem. Each of the following disorders could be the underlying cause for this patient's symptoms EXCEPT?**

❏ A Cystic fibrosis

❏ B Immotile cilia syndrome (Kartagener's syndrome)

❏ C Alpha-1-antitrypsin deficiency

❏ D IgM deficiency

❏ E Glucose-6-phosphate dehydrogenase deficiency

14.17 **The main limiting feature of spiral computed tomographic scanning for pulmonary embolism is?**

❏ A High level of artefacts due to unavoidable chest movement during respiration

❏ B Low sensitivity for detecting pulmonary emboli in main pulmonary arteries

❏ C Technical difficulty in passing a catheter into the pulmonary artery

❏ D Long scanning time

❏ E Low sensitivity for detecting pulmonary emboli in subsegmental pulmonary arteries

14.18 A 50-year-old hospital porter is an inpatient on the surgical ward after a routine cholecystectomy. He normally smokes 30 cigarettes a day. Two days after the operation he begins to spike fevers and expectorate green phlegm. A CXR shows lobar consolidation in his right lung. He has O_2 saturations of 85% on air. The surgical consultant asks you to assess him and start him on some antibiotics. Which one of the following treatments would you choose?

- ❏ A   Penicillin + Macrolide
- ❏ B   Cephalosporin alone
- ❏ C   Quinolone alone
- ❏ D   Cephalosporin + aminoglycoside
- ❏ E   Penicillin + Flucloxacillin + Macrolide

14.19 A sixty-year-old lady is seen every six months in the Chest Clinic for follow-up for her cryptogenic fibrosing alveolitis. Despite several prolonged courses of corticosteroids her lung function continues to deteriorate. You organise a repeat set of PFTs before starting her on a course of cyclophosphamide. Which one of the results below would best fit this patient?

Options (expressed as % predicted values)

- ❏ A FEV_1 60   FVC 65   ratio 90%   Va 60   KCO 60
- ❏ B FEV_1 60   FVC 65   ratio 90%   Va 85   KCO 130
- ❏ C FEV_1 65   FVC 85   ratio 70%   Va 60   KCO 60
- ❏ D FEV_1 65   FVC 85   ratio 70%   Va 85   KCO 130
- ❏ E FEV_1 60   FVC 65   ratio 90%   Va 100   KCO 50

14.20 A 50-year-old van driver with a normal body mass index is referred to the Sleep Clinic because he keeps falling asleep at the wheel, having had three car crashes. His wife complains that he keeps her awake all night snoring. A sleep study confirms moderate sleep apnoea. Which one of the treatments below would be the most suitable first line therapy?

- ❏ A   Long-term oxygen therapy
- ❏ B   Mandibular advancement splinting
- ❏ C   Pharyngeal wall surgery
- ❏ D   Tracheostomy
- ❏ E   Weight loss

15: RHEUMATOLOGY AND IMMUNOLOGY

15.1 Which one of the following features is LEAST suggestive of Guillain-Barré syndrome?

❏ A Proximal muscle weakness
❏ B Areflexia
❏ C Normal cerebrospinal fluid (CSF) cell count
❏ D Acute retention of urine
❏ E Segmental demyelination on nerve conduction study

15.2 Which one of the following immunological abnormalities is LEAST encountered in patients with acquired immune deficiency syndrome (AIDS)?

❏ A Hypergammaglobulinaemia
❏ B Depletion of T4 lymphocyte
❏ C Deficient T-lymphocyte response to antigenic and mitogenic stimulus
❏ D Low absolute B-lymphocytes count
❏ E Defective natural killer (NK) cell function

15.3 Which one of the following statements with regard to bacille Calmette-Guérin (BCG) vaccine is NOT true?

❏ A The vaccine contains live attenuated human *Mycobacterium tuberculosis*
❏ B Provides up to 10 years immunity against tuberculosis
❏ C May cause regional lymphadenopathy
❏ D In areas where TB is endemic vaccination is usually offered to all neonates
❏ E Subsequent tuberculin tests give false positive results

15.4 A 19-year-old student presents with swelling of the face, hands and feet along with diffuse abdominal pain. He gives a history of recurrent episodes since he was 10 years old, at a rate of 3–4 attacks per year. Each episode would last 2–3 days. On examination swelling is observed at the above mentioned sites but there was no evidence of urticaria. Family history reveals a history of similar episodes in the mother since childhood and in the elder brother who died of respiratory distress at the age of eight years during a similar attack. Which one of the following tests would be considered MOST helpful in establishing the diagnosis?

- ❏ A Eosinophil count in the blood
- ❏ B Prick (puncture) skin test
- ❏ C Radioallergosorbent test (RAST)
- ❏ D C1 esterase inhibitor (C1INH)
- ❏ E IgE levels

15.5 A 74-year-old-man is seen in the preoperative assessment clinic prior to a right total hip replacement scheduled in eight weeks time. He had a recent chest infection and suffered chronic joint pain and prostatism for many years. On examination there were few chest signs and the musculoskeletal examination revealed evidence of severe arthritis in the right hip and base of the thumb. The prostate is firm and enlarged. It was thought that he was fit to have the operation. However, the blood tests showed raised immunoglobulins and the immune electrophoresis identified an M-protein of the IgG type at 2.5 g/dl. Further tests reveal no lytic bone lesions on skeletal survey and no Bence-Jones proteinuria. The bone profile and the prostate specific antigen were within normal limits. The MOST likely underlying disease is?

- ❏ A Carcinoma of the prostate
- ❏ B Multiple myeloma
- ❏ C Rheumatoid arthritis
- ❏ D Monoclonal gammopathies of undetermined significance (MGUS)
- ❏ E Waldenström's macroglobulinaemia

15.6   **Which one of the following is NOT true regarding inflammatory indicators?**

❏   A   The erythrocyte sedimentation rate (ESR) is increased in hypoalbuminaemia

❏   B   The C-reactive protein (CRP) levels are elevated in acute myocardial infarction

❏   C   A rise in plasma viscosity (PV) is primarily due to an increase in haematocrit concentration

❏   D   The PV test is generally more specific and sensitive than the ESR test

❏   E   The CRP results are basically not affected by current steroid therapy

15.7   **Absent immune deposits on immunohistochemical analysis of renal tissue is characteristic of which one of the following renal disorders?**

❏   A   Systemic lupus erythematosus
❏   B   Henoch-Schönlein nephritis
❏   C   Goodpasture's disease
❏   D   Wegener's granulomatosis
❏   E   Buerger's disease

15.8   **Which one of the following is true regarding the immune system?**

❏   A   Class II major histocompatibility complex (MHC) antigens are present on virtually all human cell types

❏   B   The liver clears IgM-sensitised erythrocytes

❏   C   IL-2 is produced exclusively by T-lymphocytes

❏   D   The active complement component C5a stimulates the activation of the alternative complement pathway

❏   E   Erythrocyte destruction in paroxysmal nocturnal haemoglobinuria (PNH) takes place within the liver

15.9 **Which one of the following is rarely observed in essential mixed cryoglobulinaemia (EMC)?**

❑ A Positive rheumatoid factor
❑ B Palpable purpura
❑ C Glomerulonephritis
❑ D Cold intolerance
❑ E Hepatitis C infection

15.10 **Which one of the following statements BEST describes a patient with primary Raynaud's phenomena?**

❑ A More common in middle aged females
❑ B Digital gangrene is a frequent complication
❑ C Anti-nuclear antibody is positive in 70% of cases
❑ D Nail fold capillary scope shows dilated vessels
❑ E Fingers are symmetrically involved during an attack

15.11 **Which one of the following types of arthritis is the MOST common type of psoriatic arthropathy?**

❑ A Distal interphalangeal (DIP) joint disease
❑ B Arthritis mutilans
❑ C Peripheral symmetric polyarthropathy
❑ D Peripheral asymmetric oligoarthropathy
❑ E Psoriatic spondylitis

15.12 **Which one of the following is LEAST characteristic about the laboratory findings in the antiphospholipid syndrome?**

❑ A Positive Venereal Disease Research Laboratory test (VDRL)
❑ B Positive anticardiolipin antibodies
❑ C Prolonged activated partial thromboplastin time (APTT)
❑ D Elevated low density lipoprotein (LDL)
❑ E Thrombocytopenia

15.13 **Which one of the following clinical findings is LEAST characteristic of systemic sclerosis?**

❏ A Pulmonary hypertension is usually due to recurrent pulmonary embolism
❏ B The ESR is usually within normal limits
❏ C Alveolar cell carcinoma of the lung is a recognised complication
❏ D Visceral disease without cutaneous involvement
❏ E Skin thickening is characteristically proximal to the metacarpophalangeal joints

15.14 **Which one of the following features is MOST suggestive of gonococcal arthritis?**

❏ A Monoarthritis at the outset of the disease
❏ B Tenosynovitis
❏ C Episcleritis
❏ D Cloudy synovial fluid with a white cell count of < 800/mm^3
❏ E Fever

15.15 **A 36-year-old woman with an eight month history of Raynaud's phenomenon presents to the emergency room with new onset precordial chest pain. Physical examination reveals a pericardial friction rub and her CPK is elevated 5 times above the upper normal limit, but the MB isoenzyme is negative. The immunology profile reveals a positive ANA test at 1:640 with a speckled staining pattern. The MOST appropriate immunology test at this stage is?**

❏ A Anti-double-stranded DNA (Anti-dsDNA)
❏ B Anti-ribonucleoprotein (anti-RNP antibody)
❏ C Anti-centromere antibody
❏ D Rheumatoid factor
❏ E Anti-neutrophil cytoplasmic antibody (ANCA)

15.16 **Chondrocalcinosis is associated with each of the following disorders EXCEPT?**

❏ A Hyperparathyroidism
❏ B Addison's disease
❏ C Haemochromatosis
❏ D Hypothyroidism
❏ E Gout

15.17 **A 70-year-old female has a 20-year history of rheumatoid arthritis. A year ago her gold therapy was discontinued because it was found to be ineffective in controlling her arthritis. She was started and then maintained on D-penicillamine (375 mg). Two weeks ago she noticed increased difficulty in climbing stairs. Her husband who accompanied her added that he had to wash her hair in the last four days. On examination, she has synovial swelling at the MCPs and PIPs of both hands as well as both knees. The neck and shoulder movement were very restricted. Neurological assessment reveals grade 3/5 weakness in both upper and lower muscle groups, touch and pinprick sensation were reported intact, tendon reflexes were normal, the Babinski sign was positive bilaterally. The MOST probable cause of her recent weakness is?**

- ❏ A Spinal cord compression due to cervical myelopathy from atlanto-axial subluxation
- ❏ B D-penicillamine induced myasthenia gravis
- ❏ C Peripheral neuropathy associated rheumatoid arthritis
- ❏ D Parasagittal cerebral rheumatoid nodule
- ❏ E Generalised weakness due to disuse muscle atrophy secondary to chronic arthritis

15.18 **A 32-year-old man is referred with bouts of low back pain waking him at night for about six months. The pain is localised to the lower lumbar region and the buttock. He has changed his job from working in a warehouse doing heavy lifting to clerical tasks. He has to wake himself an hour or two earlier to loosen up so he can get to work on time. Past medical history revealed a malignant skin melanoma surgically removed two years earlier. The MOST probable diagnosis in this case is?**

- ❏ A Intervertebral disc prolapse and sciatica
- ❏ B Spinal canal stenosis
- ❏ C Ankylosing spondylitis
- ❏ D Melanoma recurrence and spread to vertebrae
- ❏ E Osteomyelitis of the lower lumbar vertebra

15.19 A 66-year-old lady has sustained two vertebral fractures following minor trauma and is diagnosed with osteoporosis. Initially she is treated with biphosphonate but because of side-effects the treatment is stopped. You are considering raloxifene as an alternative therapy. In your advice to the patient you should inform her that this therapy would?

❏ A Improve the bone mineral density in the spine and hips
❏ B Increase the risk of breast cancer
❏ C Cause vaginal bleeding at the end of each month of therapy
❏ D Increase the high density lipoprotein (HDL) levels
❏ E Increase the risk of clotting

15.20 A 50-year-old man is referred with a two-week history of fever, arthralgia and weight loss. During his hospital stay he develops epigastric pain and notices difficulty dorsiflexing his left great toe. Blood pressure is 160/95 mmHg. Laboratory studies reveal Hb 10 g/dl, MCV 98 fl, erythrocyte sedimentation rate (ESR) 100 mm/h, and polymorphonuclear leucocytosis. Chest X-ray is clear. Which one of the following is the MOST likely diagnosis?

❏ A Wegener's granulomatosus
❏ B Systemic lupus erythematosus
❏ C Polyarteritis nodosa
❏ D Polymyalgia rheumatica
❏ E Churg-Strauss syndrome

15.21 A 54-year-old woman has been experiencing increased pain and stiffness in her hands, wrists, upper arms, shoulders and calves for two years. She describes transient swelling at the wrists. She is frequently roused from sleep by pain and complains of marked fatigue with little stiffness sometimes associated with tingling in the hands, arms and feet. Review of systems reveal increasing urinary urgency and recurrent attacks of headaches. On examination there is no significant abnormality apart from multiple tender spots over the spine and limbs. Blood tests reveal a white blood cell count of 4 x 10^9/l and a platelet count of 167 x 10^9/l. The erythrocyte sedimentation rate is 20 mm/h. The rheumatoid factor is negative and the ANA test comes back positive at 1:40. The creatine kinase and thyroid function test are within normal limits. Which one of the following is the MOST probable diagnosis?

- ❏ A   Systemic lupus erythematosus
- ❏ B   Fibromyalgia syndrome
- ❏ C   Chronic fatigue syndrome
- ❏ D   Hypothyroidism
- ❏ E   Depression

15.22 Which one of the following statements regarding neuropathic (Charcot) joints is true?

- ❏ A   Diabetes mellitus is the most common cause
- ❏ B   In children it usually complicates poliomyelitis
- ❏ C   The joint often looks normal on clinical examination
- ❏ D   Syringomyelia predominantly affects the knees
- ❏ E   Joint replacement is the treatment of choice

15.23 Which one of the following disorders is LEAST associated with positive ANCA test?

- ❏ A   Wegener's granulomatosis
- ❏ B   Polyarteritis nodosa
- ❏ C   Churg-Strauss syndrome
- ❏ D   Microscopic polyangiitis
- ❏ E   Idiopathic necrotising glomerulonephritis

15.24 **Which one of the following is LEAST associated with hyperuricaemia?**

❏ A Thiazide diuretic therapy
❏ B Alcoholism
❏ C Polycythaemia rubra vera
❏ D Eclampsia of pregnancy
❏ E Psoriasis

16: STATISTICS

16.1 **Which one of the following statements concerning the distribution curve is NOT accurate?**

❏ A The mean is the sum of all the scores divided by the number of scores

❏ B The mean is a good measure of central tendency in skewed distributions

❏ C The mean is higher than the median in positively skewed distributions

❏ D When there is an even number of numbers, the median is the mean of the two middle numbers

❏ E Many distributions have more than one mode

16.2 **In a study the odds of disease in the group who smoke is 0.25. This means which one of the following:**

❏ A Smoking causes disease

❏ B For every 4 who smoke, 1 has the disease

❏ C For every 5 who smoke, 1 has the disease

❏ D The disease occurs 4 times more often in those who smoke

❏ E A larger sample is needed

16.3 **A study is designed to assess the safety of recombinant human erythropoietin (rhEPO) when used in premature infants of less than 33 weeks gestation to reduce postnatal haemoglobin decline. Out of 31 infants given the treatment none suffered serious side-effects. What should be concluded from this study?**

❏ A rhEPO is safe

❏ B rhEPO is safe when used in dosages used in this study

❏ C Nothing conclusive can be said, a larger study is needed

❏ D rhEPO does not cause serious side-effects when used in moderate doses

❏ E Premature infants of less than 33 weeks gestation can safely be given rhEPO

16.4 **Blood pressure is normally distributed. For a sample of 100 Asian women the average blood pressure is 50, standard deviation = 5, standard error = ½. Which one of the following statements is correct?**

❑ A Approximately 95% of Asian women have blood pressures in the range (45,55)
❑ B We are approximately 95% confident that the population average blood pressure for Asian women lies in the interval (49, 51)
❑ C Blood pressure measurement in Asian women is not informative
❑ D 10% of Asian women have blood pressure below 40 mmHg
❑ E The mean blood pressure of Asian women must lie within the range (49, 51)

16.5 **The average weight of a group of 100 patients is 60 kg, standard deviation 5 kg. Weights are normally distributed. The standard error of the weights is which one of the following?**

❑ A 12 kg
❑ B 0.6 kg
❑ C 5 kg
❑ D Larger than the standard deviation
❑ E Smaller than the standard deviation

1: BASIC SCIENCES: ANSWERS AND EXPLANATIONS

1.1   B: Testes
The superficial inguinal lymph nodes drain the tissues of the following structures.
- Lower limb
- Lower abdominal wall
- External genitalia
- Perineum
- Lower part of the anal canal
- Uterus by means of lymphatics that follow the round ligament.

The testes lymphatics are drained to the abdominal and para-aortic lymph nodes.

1.2   C: Ischaemic heart disease
Apoptosis is defined as 'programmed cell death' which occurs in isolated cells with no inflammatory reaction as opposed to necrosis. It is a crucial process in embryogenesis where tissue building, replacement and moulding are at their peak. Unopposed apoptosis with progressive destruction of specific groups of nerve cells is considered to be one mechanism that ultimately leads to Alzheimer's disease. On the other hand, inhibition of apoptosis with prolonged cell survival may have a determinant role in the induction of autoimmunity (prolonging immune competent cell survival). Similarly, in lung cancer, genetic abnormalities such as mutation of p53 oncogenes can lead to loss of tumour suppression function, inhibition of apoptosis and increased cellular proliferation. Recent investigation of bone marrow myeloid progenitor cells in myelodysplasia and cyclic neutropenia suggests that intramedullary apoptosis is a central feature regulating cell loss in this disorder. In ischaemic heart disease the pathogenesis involves cell death due to necrosis and is associated with local inflammatory reaction.

1.3   E: Transforming growth factor-beta (TGF-beta) inhibits other cytokine production
Cytokines are hormone-like proteins that enable the immune cells to communicate. They play an important role in initiation, perpetuation and subsequent down regulation of immune response. In addition to immune cells they are also produced by non-immune cells such as fibroblast and endothelial cells. Interleukin-6 (IL-6) enhances the liver to produce the acute phase reactant proteins but not albumin which is not an acute phase reactant. IL-2 produced by T-cells increases expression of its own receptor on T-cells and markedly enhances T-cell proliferation. Distinct subsets of helper T-cells have been identified by virtue of the cytokines that they

produce, Th1 cells regulate delayed type hypersensitivity reaction and Th2 cells mediate allergic and antibody response.

1.4 E: Sildenafil (*Viagra*) doubles the sperm count three months after initiation of treatment

Normal ejaculate volume ranges from 2 to 6 ml. The normal ranges of sperm concentration is 20–200 million per millilitre and up to 20% are morphologically abnormal. More than 60% of sperms examined within one hour after ejaculation are motile. In any individual, sperm counts exhibit extreme variability and are often temporarily suppressed by factors such as fever. Sildenafil (*Viagra*) has been licensed for the treatment of impotence. It causes vasodilatation of the corpora cavernosa blood vessels and hence increases the blood flow and maintains erection in the penis. *Viagra* has no direct effect on sperm count or fertility.

1.5 E: Angiotensin II

Renin is a glycoprotein of 274 amino acids and is produced in the juxtaglomerular cells of the afferent renal arteriole. It will convert angiotensinogen to angiotensin I. It is also stimulated by lowering blood pressure. Angiotensin II and vasopressin inhibit renin release.

1.6 B: The abductor pollicis brevis

The median nerve supplies the following structures in the hand:
- The abductor pollicis brevis, flexor pollicis brevis, opponens pollicis
- The lateral two lumbricales
- The skin of the lateral three and half fingers.

The ulnar nerve supplies all the interossei and the rest of the hand muscles.

1.7 A: Synthesised in the posterior pituitary

Arginine vasopressin is synthesised in the supraoptic and paraventricular nuclei of the hypothalamus. V2 receptors induce its antidiuretic effect. It stimulates ACTH release and increases circulating haemophilic factor VIII and von Willebrand factor. By stimulating V1 receptors it causes vaso-constriction of splanchnic, renal and coronary vessels as well as promoting glycogenolysis.

1.8 E: Endothelial cells

Tissue macrophages are either fixed or wandering macrophages. The fixed macrophages include Kupffer cells, microglial cells (CNS), mesangial cells (kidney), osteoblasts, in addition to the macrophages of the Reticulo-endothelial system. Wandering macrophages include macrophages of the serosal cavities (pleura, peritoneum, pericardium) and alveolar macrophages.

1.9   A: Alveolar hypoventilation

Physiological acclimatisation starts at about 7000 ft (2100 m). The partial pressure of atmospheric O_2 reduces with altitude. Pulmonary ventilation and perfusion increase, plasma volume reduces and renal excretion of bicarbonate increases. These changes serve to maintain arterial O_2 tension. Erythrocyte production increases; the haemoglobin and haematocrit increase. Above 1400 ft the heart rate, cardiac output and pulmonary artery pressure increase. Alveolar hypoventilation, hypoxia and cyanosis are features of chronic mountain sickness when the physiological response of acclimatisation is no longer maintained.

1.10   B: Sulphate

Buffers are substances or solutions which accept a proton or hydroxyl group with very little change in overall pH.

Blood buffers include bicarbonate, phosphate, protein and haemoglobin.

1.11   C: Stroke volume

During exercise, increased oxygen consumption and increased venous return to the heart result in an increase in cardiac output and an increase in blood flow to both skeletal muscle and coronary circulation, when oxygen utilization is greatest. The increase in cardiac output is due to an increase in both heart rate and stroke volume. Systemic arterial pressure also increases in response to the increase in cardiac output. However, the fall in total peripheral resistance, which is caused by dilatation of the blood vessels within the exercising muscles, results in a decrease in diastolic blood pressure. The pulmonary vessels undergo passive dilatation as more blood flows into the pulmonary circulation. As a result, pulmonary vascular resistance decreases. The decrease in venous compliance, caused by sympathetic stimulation, helps to maintain ventricular filling during diastole.

1.12   E: Confusion and coma often ensue when serum sodium approaches 125 mmol/l

In heart failure, reduced cardiac output will cause reduced renal blood flow, increase of aldosterone secretion and sympathetic activity which results in salt and water retention by the kidneys. ADH is increased in heart failure causing further limitation of free water excretion. Together with the increased thirst in patients with advanced heart failure, this leads to a hyponatraemic state that is a particularly ominous prognostic sign in heart failure. Hyponatraemia in liver disease is typically due to a combination of reduced renal clearance of free water and administration of excessive free water in the form of dextrose solutions. Mineralocorticoid deficiency causes increased urinary clearance of sodium with volume contraction and increased ADH, which reduces free water excretion. The clinical features of hyponatraemia generally manifest when the serum sodium concentration falls to 120 mmol/l or less. Paraproteinaemia causes false hyponatraemia due to displacement of more fluid in the serum, which gives false readings.

1.13   A: V/Q ratio
The alveoli at the apex of the lung are larger than those at the base so their compliance is less. Because of the reduced compliance, less inspired gas goes to the apex than to the base. Also, because the apex is above the heart level, less blood flows through the apex than through the base. However, the reduction in air flow is less than the reduction in blood flow, so that the V/Q ratio at the top of the lung is greater than it is at the bottom. The increased V/Q ratio at the apex makes $PaCO_2$ lower and PaO_2 higher at the apex than they are at the base.

1.14   B: Dopamine
The pathogenesis of Parkinson's disease is multifactorial, characterised by a progressive death of heterogeneous populations of neurones particularly in the substantia nigra, resulting in a regional loss of the neurotransmitter dopamine. A 60–70% loss of neurones occurs prior to the emergence of symptoms.

1.15   B: Aschoff nodules in rheumatic fever
Pathognomonic *adj.* is a symptom or sign unique to a particular disease. The presence of such a sign or symptom allows positive diagnosis of the disease.

Although the histological diagnosis of Hodgkin's disease requires the presence of Reed-Sternberg cells, these cells are not pathognomonic of the disease and have been described in infectious mononucleosis, other viral infections and malignancies. Aschoff nodules, considered pathognomonic of rheumatic fever, consist of a central area of fibrinoid surrounded by lymphocytes, plasma cells, and large basophilic cells, some of them are multinucleated. Charcot-Leyden crystals (CLCs) have been found in many conditions associated with eosinophilia. Crystals of CLC protein in body fluids and secretions have long been considered a hallmark of eosinophil-associated allergic inflammatory diseases such as asthma, allergic rhinitis and also atopic dermatitis. Alcoholic hyaline (Mallory body) is not specific for alcoholic liver disease since it has been detected in the livers of patients with Wilson's disease, primary biliary cirrhosis, hepatic carcinoma and following jejuno-ileal bypass. The presence of non-caseating granuloma should not be construed as diagnostic of sarcoidosis until a thorough investigation of other causes of granulomatous inflammations has been conducted.

1.16   B: Exercise
Growth hormone (GH) is synthesised, stored, and secreted by the endocrine cells of the anterior pituitary. Its release is stimulated by growth hormone-releasing hormone and inhibited by somatostatin. Numerous factors serve as a stimulus for GH release, including hypoglycaemia (e.g. insulin administration), moderate to severe exercise, stress due to emotional disturbances, illness, and fever, and dopamine agonists such as bromocriptine.

1.17   B: Prostate
Tumours that have a predilection for dissemination to bone are those of the prostate (32%), breast (22%), and kidney (16%) followed by the lung and the thyroid.

1.18   C: It has a lower glucose concentration than plasma
Cerebrospinal fluid (CSF) is formed primarily in the choroid plexus by an active secretory process. It circulates in the subarachnoid space between the dura mater and pia mater and is absorbed into the circulation by the arachnoid villi. The epidural space, which lies outside the dura mater, may be used clinically for instillation of anaesthetics. CSF protein and glucose concentrations are much lower than those in the plasma.

1.19   E: Renin
Aldosterone is a mineralocorticoid secreted by the zona glomerulosa layer of the adrenal gland, its main action is on the kidneys causing sodium and water retention. Renin and angiotensin II stimulate aldosterone production. An increased serum potassium level stimulates, and a reduced potassium level inhibits its release, as little as 0.1 Meq/L change will affect aldosterone secretion independent of sodium or angiotensin II. ACTH has a transient stimulatory effect and chronic ACTH deficiency rarely blunts aldosterone production. Hyponatraemia reduces and hypernatraemia increases aldosterone release, these influences are probably mediated through the effect of renin. Dopamine agonist (bromocriptine) inhibits aldosterone secretion while dopamine antagonists stimulate its release.

1.20 A: It inhibits angiogenesis hence the prominent anti-tumour activity

The main sources of TNF are the activated cells of the monocyte-phagocytic system and, to a lesser extent, antigen-stimulated T-cells, natural killer (NK) cells and activated mast cells. TNF plays a central role in the immune system and appears to be particularly critical for innate immunity. It is an important mediator of local inflammation and appears to be vital in keeping infections localised. TNF results in local activation of vascular endothelium, release of nitric oxide with vasodilatation, increased vascular permeability, increased expression of adhesion molecules on the endothelium of blood vessels, and increased expression of class II major histocompatibility molecules. The result is recruitment of inflammatory cells, immunoglobulins, and complement. It promotes angiogenesis. Clearly, TNF has a central role in the pathological inflammatory response associated with rheumatoid arthritis. Evidence to support this statement includes excess TNF levels in the serum; the correlation between an abundance of macrophage products (TNF, interleukins 1, 6, and 8) in the synovial tissue and fluid, with the severity and activity of disease; and, most important, the consistent improvement in disease activity, both symptomatically and radiographically, when therapy is directed against TNF.

1.21 E: Coronary

Hypoxia activates chemoreceptors causing a sympathetic vasoconstrictor response in the skin, skeletal muscle and splanchnic beds. In contrast, in the presence of hypoxia the coronary, cerebral and renovascular beds undergo vasodilatation, thus permitting the redistribution of blood to the vital organs with higher oxygen demand.

1.22 A: Composed of smooth involuntary muscle and central tendon

The diaphragm is composed of skeletal muscle and a central tendon. When the muscle contracts the diaphragm descends, paradoxical upward movement of the diaphragm and inward movement of the abdominal wall during inspiration occur when there is bilateral paralysis of the diaphragm. Normally the right dome of the diaphragm is higher than the left one. The diaphragm is higher on the paralysed side on X-ray examination. Each hemi-diaphragm is supplied by a correspondent phrenic nerve, hiccough is believed to be due to mechanical or metabolic irritation of the phrenic nerve that causes spasmodic contraction of the diaphragm.

1.23 B: Squamous

Hypercalcaemia is the most common metabolic abnormality associated with cancer.

Parathyroid hormone-related peptide (PTH-rP) has emerged as the main mediator of hypercalcaemia not only in squamous cell tumours (e.g. lung, skin, head and neck, cervix, vulva) but also in breast, renal, ovarian carcinomas, pancreatic islet cell tumours, phaeochromocytomas and haematologic malignancies such as leukaemias, lymphomas, and multiple myeloma. In general, PTH-rP is a humoral factor that circulates in the bloodstream and is transported to bone, where it stimulates bone resorption through the PTH/PTH-rP receptor. However, it may also be locally produced by tumour cells that have metastasised to bone, often in conjunction with cytokines such as interleukin-6 (IL-6). PTH-rP, IL-6, and other factors synergistically stimulate osteoclast-mediated bone resorption, as well as production by osteoclasts of tumour growth factors such as transforming growth factor beta (TGF-beta). TGF-beta in turn stimulates further PTH-rP production, thus setting in motion and amplifying an ineluctable process of tumour growth and hypercalcemia. Therefore, by inhibiting osteoclasts, bisphosphonates such as pamidronate not only decrease hypercalcemia and skeletal morbidity, but also tumour burden. One of the most exciting findings in this field in recent years is the fact that bisphosphonates may actually improve quality of life and prolong survival in patients with breast cancer and multiple myeloma.

Tumor cell type hormone

Neuroendocrine	adrenocorticotropic hormone (ACTH)
	arginine vasopressin (AVP)
	corticotropin-releasing factor (CRF)
	growth hormone-releasing hormone (GHRH)
	somatostatin
	calcitonin
Squamous	parathyroid hormone-related hormone (PTH-rP)
Large cell	human chorionic gonadotropin (hCG)
Mesenchymal	insulin-like growth factor II (IGF-II)
	phosphaturic factor

1.24   D: Homozygous C2 deficiency is associated with systemic lupus erythematosus

Only IgG and IgM can activate the classic pathway, as other antibody classes are not capable of binding C1 complement. In hereditary angioedema the cause is C1INH (C1 esterase inhibitor) deficiency and not C1 complement deficiency. C1, C2, and C4 are typically normal when the alternative pathway is activated. Inherited deficiency of C1q, C2, and C4 is associated with high incidence of autoimmune diseases (SLE, vasculitis) while deficiency of complement C5, C6, C7 and C8 is associated with selective propensity for developing disseminated neisserial infection. Renal disease in scleroderma resembles the nephropathy of malignant hypertension; hypocomplementaemia is not a feature of this disorder.

1.25   C: The vast majority of obese individuals have markedly elevated plasma leptin concentrations

The discovery of leptin continued the hormonal link between the adipocyte and the brain. Leptin is mainly secreted by the adipocyte, circulates in part while linked to binding proteins, and acts in specific regions of the brain (hypothalamus) to regulate appetite and energy balance. Daily injections of leptin decreased appetite and body weight in both *ob/ob* mice and wild-type mice and increased energy expenditure in lean new-born Zucker rats. Leptin deficiency caused genetic obesity in *ob/ob* mice as well as in a recently described family kindred.The vast majority of obese individuals have markedly elevated plasma leptin concentrations when compared to lean individuals. In fact, plasma leptin concentrations strongly correlate with the percentage of body fat and leptin levels are reduced in obese subjects who lose weight. A higher set point of the cerebral adipostat present in obese individuals may be the result of a relative or absolute insensitivity to leptin. This has led to the notion that 'leptin' resistance underlies most cases of obesity.

1.26 E: Lowers high blood cholesterol

Epidemiological and clinical studies have shown that potassium intake has an important role in regulating blood pressure in both the general population and individuals with high blood pressure. High potassium intake may have other beneficial effects independent of its effect on blood pressure e.g. reducing the risk of stroke, preventing the development of renal vascular, glomerular, and tubular damage. Increasing potassium intake reduces calcium excretion and causes a positive calcium balance that may be associated in the longer term with a higher bone mass. A reduction in calcium excretion is associated with reduced risk of kidney stones. Increasing serum potassium concentrations reduces the risk of ventricular arrhythmias in patients with ischaemic heart disease, heart failure, and left ventricular hypertrophy. High potassium intake has no effect on blood cholesterol levels.

1.27 B: 1500 mg/day of calcium, 400 to 800 U/day of vitamin D

Adequate calcium and vitamin D intake should be a part of the prevention and treatment of osteoporosis. Dietary intake of calcium should be 800–1000 mg/day in childhood through early adulthood, 1000–1200 mg/day in the middle years, and 1500 mg/day in the elderly. If osteoporosis is established, the treatment includes 1500 mg/day of calcium and 400–800 U/day of vitamin D.

1.28 E: Levels are typically normal in Di George syndrome

IgG is the only antibody that crosses the placenta. IgM has the highest molecular weight, however, IgG has the highest concentration in plasma. All immunoglobulins are synthesised by lymphocytes. Di George syndrome is characterised by dysmorphogenesis of the third and the fourth pharyngeal pouches leading to hypoplasia or aplasia of the thymus and the parathyroid gland. It manifests as hypocalcaemic fits in neonate, a low T-lymphocyte cell count, high B-lymphocyte cell count and typically normal immunoglobulin levels.

1.29   B: Anti-platelet
COX-2 inhibition is responsible for the analgesic and the anti-inflammatory effect of Celecoxib and Rofecoxib (known as Coxibs) which appear indistinguishable from that of several standard NSAIDs. The renal effects of Coxibs are similar to nonselective traditional NSAIDs. They cause sodium and water retention; both are associated with increased incidence of peripheral oedema and worsening of pre-existing hypertension. Coxibs can cause bronchospasm and rarely, angio-oedema, as with other NSAIDs. Unlike older nonselective COX inhibitors, COX-2 inhibitors do not decrease the production of thromboxane in platelets and therefore do not inhibit platelet aggregation or increase bleeding time. As normal platelet function is preserved in patients on selective COX-2 inhibitors, patients requiring cardioprotective anti-platelet therapy should continue low-dose aspirin.

1.30   D: Increase in insulin-mediated glucose uptake in muscle
In the shock state, an increase in membrane permeability to sodium and water, causing cellular swelling is noted initially. This is followed by an increase in sodium/potassium ATPase activity in an attempt to drive sodium out of the cell. Increased membrane ATPase activity eventually leads to the depletion of ATP and cyclic AMP. The latter may lead to alterations in the cellular response to insulin, glucagon, catecholamines, and other hormones. In animals that have been subjected to haemorrhagic shock, insulin-mediated glucose uptake by muscle is reduced.

2: CARDIOLOGY: ANSWERS AND EXPLANATIONS

2.1 E: The mean pulmonary artery pressure is more than 25 mmHg at rest

One of the diagnostic criteria includes a mean pulmonary artery pressure of more than 25 mmHg at rest or more than 30 mmHg with exercise. Recurrent thromboembolism is one cause of secondary pulmonary hypertension (not primary). Fenfluramine, cocaine inhalation and HIV infection can cause pulmonary vascular disease with clinical and pathological features similar to those of primary pulmonary hypertension. The familial form is inherited as autosomal dominant. The medium period of survival is two to three years after the diagnosis. Recent improvement in diagnosis and newer forms of treatment have improved survival, but the prognosis is generally very poor and most patients gradually succumb to progressive right-sided heart failure.

2.2 A: Atrial septal defect (ASD)

Paradoxical splitting of the second heart sound due to
* late A2 (aortic component of the second heart sound) which occurs in LBBB, aortic stenosis and PDA.
* early P2 (pulmonary component of the second heart sound) which occurs in type B WPW syndrome. Atrial septal defect (ASD) causes wide splitting and not paradoxical splitting of the second heart sound.

Normal heart sounds: |————-(^{A2} || ^{P2})————|
            first   second   first
Paradoxical splitting of the second heart sound:
            |————-(^{P2} || ^{A2})————|
            first   second   first

2.3 A: The coarctation is proximal to the left subclavian artery origin if the right arm blood pressure is significantly higher than in the left arm

The commonest site of discrete obstruction of the aortic lumen is just distal to the origin of the left subclavian artery. The systolic arterial pressure in the arms exceeds that in the leg. If the systolic arterial pressure in the right arm is higher than that of the left arm by more than 30 mmHg, the left subclavian is involved in the coarctation. Continuous murmur over the thoracic spine usually originate from small, tight coarctation (< 2 mm). Other cardiac malformations are frequent, the commonest being a bicuspid aortic valve. Notching of the inferior border of the ribs from collateral vessels is common and usually manifest in adults and older children. Patients with coarctation are at high risk of subacute bacterial endocarditis and should be strongly advised about antibiotic prophylaxis.

2.4   C: Echocardiogram is diagnostic in most cases

Atrial myxoma is a benign tumour of the heart. Approximately 75% originate in the left atrium. The clinical features are characterised by a triad of embolism, intracardiac obstruction and constitutional symptoms. The clinical signs can mimic mitral stenosis and the murmur may vary with body position. Fragments of tumour easily break off but do not grow in its peripheral sites. After complete and careful removal of the tumour recurrence is very rare.

2.5   C: If *Streptococcus bovis* endocarditis is diagnosed a thorough investigation of the colon is indicated

Streptococcus bovis is often associated with colonic carcinomas and polyps. The most common cause of negative blood culture in a patient with infective endocarditis is prior antimicrobial therapy. Early prosthetic valve endocarditis occurs within 60 days of valve placement. *Staphylococcus epidermidis* is the leading cause of early valve endocarditis. Prophylaxis is probably not required to cover for endocarditis, cardiac catheterisation, insertion of pacemaker, broncho-scopy, endoscopy, normal vaginal delivery and dilatation and curettage. Cystoscopy is one of the procedures that requires antibiotic prophylaxis.

2.6   E: Digoxin therapy

Prolonged QT interval   is usually associated with the use of class I antiarrhythmic drugs (quinidine, procaine amide) and other drugs like phenytoin and tricyclic antidepressants. Electrolyte imbalance especially hypokalaemia and hypomagnesaemia can cause prolonged QT interval. Other causes include acute myocardial infarction, myocarditis, hypo-thermia and amiodarone therapy. Digoxin effect is characterised by a short QT interval.

2.7   A: *Staphylococcus aureus* is the most frequent causative agent

Staphylococcus aureus alone accounts for 50–70% of cases. Large vegetations are typical. Abscesses in the fibro-cardiac skeleton tissue or the myocardium are much more likely to be found in acute bacterial endocarditis than subacute bacterial endocarditis. They might cause conduction defects if they are adjacent to the fibres of the conduction system.

2.8   C: Measurement of pulmonary artery wedge pressure

The adult respiratory distress syndrome (ARDS) is a clinical triad of hypoxaemia, diffuse lung infiltrates, and reduced lung compliance not attributable to congestive cardiac failure. This has been reported as a complication of apparently unrelated conditions. Examples include sepsis, lung contusion and drug overdose. Increase in lung water in ARDS occurs as a result of an increase in alveolar capillary permeability and is not due to an increase in hydrostatic forces. Clinically and radiographically, ARDS closely resembles severe haemodynamic pulmonary oedema due to heart failure. The distinction between these disorders is often apparent from the clinical circumstances associated with the onset of respiratory distress, whereas differentiation by radiographic means alone is often extremely difficult. As in cardiac pulmonary oedema, the increase in lung water associated with ARDS produces interstitial oedema and alveolar collapse, and so the affected lung becomes stiff and the alveolar-arterial oxygen tension difference widens. The central venous pressure and ejection fraction may alter but would not reflect the underlying pathophysiological mechanism. A Swan-Ganz catheter should be placed if the mechanism of oedema formation cannot be discerned with confidence. A pulmonary capillary wedge pressure < 18 mmHg favours acute lung injury over haemodynamic pulmonary oedema. In clinical practice, determination of pulmonary artery wedge pressure is the most helpful discriminate between ARDS and cardiac failure.

2.9   B: The click and murmur occur later in systole when the patient stands

The systolic click-murmur syndrome is associated with mitral valve prolapse. It occurs in approximately 4% of the normal asymptomatic population. It can place excessive stress on the papillary muscles and lead to ischaemia and chest pain. Although often associated with inferior T-wave changes, the systolic click-murmur syndrome only occasionally results in an ischaemic response to exercise. On standing or during the Valsalva manoeuvre, as ventricular volume gets smaller, the click and murmur move earlier in systole. Echocardiography reveals mid-systolic prolapse of the posterior mitral leaflet or, on occasion, both mitral leaflets into the left atrium. Asymmetrical hypertrophy of the interventricular septum is a feature of hypertrophic obstructive cardiomyopathy (HOCM). Infective endocarditis prophylaxis is necessary for those patients with a murmur; an isolated mid-systolic click does not merit them.

2.10   A: Bicuspid aortic valve disease
Approximately 1% of the general population has a bicuspid aortic valve defect. The bicuspid aortic valve may function normally throughout life, with late stenosis resulting from fibrocalcific thickening. Aortic stenosis resulting from bicuspid valve disease occurs from increasing rigidity of the abnormal aortic valve and increasing calcification. The congenital form of bicuspid valve disease is conjoined anteriorly.

2.11   A: Ischaemic heart disease
Mitral stenosis, tricuspid stenosis and secondary pulmonary hypertension due to pulmonary embolism are associated with right ventricular strain and hypertrophy with partial or complete right bundle branch block. Pericarditis is not associated with bundle branch block.

2.12   C: Glomerulonephritis is due to autoimmune mechanism
Up to 15% of patients do not have a heart murmur when first examined, but nearly all will develop a murmur when the disease has run its course. In SBE the spleen often shows moderate enlargement, usually without noticeable tenderness unless there is splenic abscess or recent embolic infarction. Glomerulonephritis is caused by deposition of immune complex in the glomerular basement membrane. Mycotic aneurysms are caused by an inflammatory reaction in the arterial wall, caused by septic microemboli to the vasovasorum, or to impaction of an infected embolus in the arterial lumen. The site most often involved is the proximal aorta, including the sinuses of Valsalva. Heart failure is by far the most important adverse prognostic factor, other adverse factors include aortic valve involvement, renal failure, culture-negative disease, Gram-negative or fungal infection and prosthetic valve infection.

2.13   B: A 10 mmHg drop in diastolic blood pressure toward the end of pregnancy
Despite an expansion of the plasma volume and cardiac output of 50%, mean and diastolic blood pressures fall by approximately 15% owing to a reduction in peripheral vascular resistance. Tachycardia rather than bradycardia is a recognised physiological change during pregnancy. It is a consequence of reduced peripheral vascular resistance and fall in blood pressure levels. The heart may be slightly enlarged and may be displaced outward because of the high diaphragm. A pulmonary systolic murmur from a high blood flow is common and there may be a physiological third heart sound. Diastolic murmurs are generally pathological and at the mitral area may signify mitral stenosis. The presence of pulsus alternans usually signifies advanced heart failure.

2.14   D: Ambulatory blood pressure monitoring is necessary for further treatment monitoring

This patient is hypertensive and probably has generalised atherosclerosis. The low blood pressure reading in the right arm is a direct consequence of reduced blood flow in the atherosclerosed arteries of the upper arm. The diagnosis of hypertension should be based on the arm with the highest mean blood pressure reading and this arm should be used for all subsequent BP measurement. A rise in diastolic pressure when the patient goes from the supine to the standing position is most compatible with essential hypertension; a fall, in the absence of antihypertensive medications, suggests secondary forms of hypertension.

Plasma renin activity (PRA) is significantly lower in black people compared with whites independent of age and blood pressure status. The lower PRA appears to be due to a reduction in the rate of secretion of renin as a consequence of differences in renal sodium handling between blacks and whites. The blacks are probably more sensitive to salts. Blood pressure reduction following short term sodium restriction is greater in blacks compared with whites. Beta-blockers and ACE inhibitors may not be as effective as thiazide diuretics and calcium channel blockers in controlling blood pressure in blacks. Ambulatory blood pressure monitoring is most clinically helpful and most commonly used in patients with suspected 'white-coat hypertension', but it is also helpful in patients with apparent drug resistance, hypotensive symptoms with antihypertensive medications, episodic hypertension, and autonomic dysfunction. However, this procedure should not be used indiscriminately such as in the routine evaluation of patients with suspected hypertension or monitoring response to treatment.

2.15   E: It has high negative predictive values, so a negative result completely excludes VTE

D-dimer is a plasmin-mediated fibrin breakdown product; elevated levels in the plasma imply that fibrin has formed and subsequently undergone proteolysis. Several studies have shown that in the presence of a variety of clotting disorders, including deep venous thrombosis and pulmonary embolism, elevated levels of plasma D-dimer are present. However, nonthrombotic disorders such as inflammatory disease and postoperative surgical haemostasis can also cause elevated D-dimer levels. Therefore, D-dimer assays are sensitive for deep venous thrombosis and pulmonary embolism but relatively non-specific; in other words, the presence of normal D-dimer levels helps to exclude these diseases (high negative predictive values) but the presence of elevated levels is non-diagnostic (low positive predictive values). Elevated D-dimer levels are often detected in plasma regardless of the size or the type of blood vessel involved. A ruptured Baker's cyst is associated with intense inflammatory reaction in the calf which may lead to activation of the coagulation cascade and even secondary venous thrombosis.

2.16   E: It is often regarded as a medical emergency

Acute aortic regurgitation is often regarded as a medical emergency due to the inability of the left ventricle to adapt quickly to the rapid increase in end diastolic volume caused by regurgitant blood. Causes include infective endocarditis, traumatic rupture of the aortic leaflet and aortic root dissection. In rheumatic fever, the mitral valve is commonly involved and only rarely the aortic valve. Acute aortic regurgitation usually presents with features of cardiovascular collapse and acute pulmonary oedema. The pulse pressure is normal or reduced. The S3 is often present but S4 is absent. The left ventricular size and contractility are relatively normal on echocardiography.

2.17   A: Atheroembolic disease

Although each of the mentioned options is a valid possible underlying cause behind this presentation, it is clear that the picture is more typical of atheroembolic disease. It is due to cholesterol emboli lodged in peripheral arteries, commonly as a result of angiographic or other surgical vascular procedures. Clearly the clinical features will depend on the site of embolisation. The most common clinical findings are cutaneous features, renal failure and worsening hypertension. The presence of foot pulses with gangrenous toes should suggest cholesterol embolisation. The retina provides a unique opportunity to visualise the cholesterol emboli. Renal failure may manifest as gradual deterioration of renal function following angiography or may be acute (this may mimic acute dissection of the renal artery during renal angiography). Eosinophilia, eosinophiluria, a raised ESR and hypocomplementinaemia have been found in atheroembolic disease.

2.18   B: Kussmaul's sign

An inspiratory increase in venous pressure (Kussmaul's sign) and a steep y descent in the jugular pulse are features of constrictive pericarditis. Pericardial knock in early diastole is often seen in constrictive pericarditis. Both conditions cause failure of either side of the heart and the diastolic pressure in all cardiac chambers are equal. A paradoxical pulse and prominent x trough in the jugular pulse are more common in tamponade than in constrictive pericarditis.

CLINICAL PHARMACOLOGY AND TOXICOLOGY: ANSWERS AND EXPLANATIONS

3.1   C: Punctate basophilic stippling on peripheral blood film examination

Lead poisoning could occur through ingestion, inhalation and direct skin contact. Numerous occupations entail potentially significant exposure, e.g. miners, welders, storage battery workers. Pottery workers are particularly heavily exposed. The exact pathogenesis of lead colic remains uncertain. In part it appears to be due to the direct effect of lead on intestinal smooth muscles. Lead interferes with a variety of red cell enzymes leading to red cell abnormalities which include punctuate basophilic stippling and clover leaf morphology. The peripheral neuropathy, which is seen in adult patients, is almost always exclusively motor. Interstitial nephritis is the characteristic lesion in the kidneys. A gingival blue-black or grey line is found in up to 20% of adult patients but is infrequent in children.

3.2   B: Copper

It is also used to reduce the body burden of copper in Wilson's disease.

3.3   E: CT scan of the brain identifies hypodense periventricular lesions characteristic of CO poisoning

Carbon monoxide (CO) is one of the most important causes of death from poisoning in many developed countries. The two most common sources of the gas in acute poisonings are motor vehicle exhaust fumes and smoke from a fire. A low base-line level of CO is detectable in every person. Tobacco smoke is an important source of CO. Blood CO commonly reaches a level of 10% in smokers and may even exceed 15% as compared with 1–3% in non-smokers. CO poisoning in pregnancy has an especially deleterious effect on the fetus, because of the greater sensitivity of the fetus to the harmful effect of the gas. The concentration of COHb increases slowly in the fetus and reaches a peak which is 10–15% higher than that in the mother. The exaggerated leftward shift of CO makes tissue hypoxia more severe by causing less oxygen to be released to fetal tissues. Venous blood samples are adequate, although an arterial sample allows for additional determination of coexisting acidosis. CT imaging of the head is not helpful in establishing the diagnosis of CO intoxication and is usually within normal limits. However, it may be used to rule out other conditions that might result in changes in mental status or loss of consciousness in patients presenting to an acute care facility.

3.4   D: Naloxone is the only specific opioid antagonist which reverses the effect of all opioids

Naloxone is a specific opioid antagonist. It is the only antagonist which reverses the effects of pentazocine overdosage but even very large doses are unlikely to counteract those of buprenorphine. Administration of naloxone to poisoned opioid addicts may precipitate an acute withdrawal syndrome comprising abdominal cramps, nausea, diarrhoea, piloerection and vasoconstriction. While this is distressing, it is short-lived and seldom severe. In such cases it is advisable to titrate the amount of naloxone given so that life-threatening toxicity is reserved without precipitating significant withdrawal symptoms.

It is possible that naloxone occasionally reverses the CNS toxicity of ethanol and diazepam. In patients who are not obviously addicts, an unexpected response raises the possibility of poisoning with a paracetamol/opioid formulation. The plasma paracetamol concentration should be measured urgently. Patients who have become unconscious from such combined preparations have also taken sufficient paracetamol to be at risk of severe, but preventable, liver necrosis. While intravenous administration is optimum, there are occasions when venous access is not possible. In such situations naloxone may be instilled down an endotracheal tube or given intramuscularly. Injection sublingually has been used in shocked patients.

3.5   C: Gentamycin

Antimicrobial drugs with antianaerobic activity include:
Penicillin
Cephalosporins
Erythromycin
Clindamycin
Tetracycline
Chloramphenicol
Metronidazole
Aminoglycosides, Quinoline antimicrobial drugs, aztreonam and Ceftazidime are least active against most anaerobic bacteria. These drugs are included in antimicrobial regimes for therapy of mixed infections, though their role is clearly to suppress the facultative Gram-negative components.

3.6 A: Reduces protein C levels in the blood

Warfarin competitively inhibits carboxylation of vitamin K dependent factors. Vitamin K dependent factors include: factor II; VII; IX; X ('reverse the year 1972') and protein C. The half-life of warfarin is approximately 44 hours. The level of warfarin in breast milk is too little to be of any clinical significance. Autoimmune thrombocytopenia and osteoporosis are side-effects more often encountered with heparin rather than warfarin therapy.

3.7 A: Inhibits bacterial DNA replication

Vancomycin is bactericidal against several species of Gram-positive cocci, it is less effective on Gram-negative cocci. It acts on multiplying organisms by inhibiting formation of the peptidoglycan component of the cell wall. Vancomycin is poorly absorbed from the gut and it is eliminated by the kidney. Its main side-effect is damage to the auditory portion of the VIIIth cranial nerve.

3.8 E: Acetazolamide

Acetazolamide (carbonic anhydrase inhibitor) inhibits proximal tubule bicarbonate reabsorption in a similar fashion to type II renal tubular acidosis (RTA). Amiloride acts by inhibiting the sodium channel in the collecting duct which inhibits renal acid secretion or bicarbonate reabsorption. All diuretics that promote sodium chloride loss and cause volume depletion are more likely to produce a picture of metabolic alkalosis.

3.9 B: Stimulates the pancreas to release stored insulin

Metformin is a biguanide, hence its main mode of action is to reduce absorption of carbohydrate from the gut and increase the utilisation of glucose in peripheral tissues provided insulin is present. It also reduces hepatic gluconeogenesis. It does not cause clinical hypoglycaemia in normal subjects nor in diabetics, but it does cause lactic acidosis. Unlike biguanides, sulphonylureas act primarily by stimulating the beta islet cells of the pancreas to release stored insulin.

3.10 C: Less profound antimuscarinic effect

Selective serotonin re-uptake inhibitors (SSRIs) are a group of anti-depressants that differ from tricyclic antidepressants in that they are less sedative with weak antimuscarinic effect and low cardiotoxicity. They do not cause weight gain and the gastrointestinal side-effects, namely diarrhoea, nausea and vomiting, are dose related. As with tricyclic antidepressants, caution is necessary in epileptics, and in patients taking

MAOIs a two week drug free period is necessary before commencing treatment with SSRIs.

3.11   C: Not associated with increased incidence of late leukaemia
^{131}I is administered as an oral solution or capsule of sodium ^{131}I, which is rapidly concentrated in thyroid tissue. The beta-emissions result in ablation of the gland in 6–18 weeks. The parathyroid gland is not affected because the radiation penetrates only 0.5 mm of tissue. Only 10–15% of patients fail the first radioiodine treatment and require a second or subsequent dose. Many large studies, including a prospective study of 36,000 patients, have not found an increased risk of cancer or leukaemia. It is generally accepted that there is increased risk of worsening Graves' ophthalmopathy during radioactive iodine therapy.

3.12   C: Erythromycin stearate can cause cholestasis
INH typically induces liver damage in rapid acetylators. With repeated exposure to halothane anaesthesia the intervals between exposure and clinical manifestations decrease. The mechanism of injury is not known, but immune mechanism has been invoked. All erythromycins cause cholestatic reaction in the liver except for erythromycin stearate. Chlorpromazine also induces cholestatic reaction while allopurinol, phenytoin and hydralazine usually cause liver granulomas.

3.13   E: Dipyridamole
Dipyridamole is a weak antiplatelet agent that acts by increasing the cellular concentration of cyclic adenosine monophosphate (cAMP). It inhibits the phosphodiesterase enzyme which converts cyclic adenosine monophosphate (cAMP) to inactive 5'AMP. Elevated levels of cAMP and cGMP inhibit activation and aggregation of platelets. Aspirin is a potent inhibitor of platelet cyclo-oxygenase. This is an enzyme that converts arachidonic acid to thromboxane A_2 (TxA_2), a strong platelet agonist. Because the platelet has no protein synthetic apparatus the effects of aspirin are irreversible and last for the life of the platelet (8–10 days). The antiplatelet effect of clopidogrel like ticlopidine, results from antagonism of a platelet ADP receptor, P2T, resulting in inhibition of platelet activation. This antagonism is non-competitive, irreversible, and results in 50–70% inhibition of fibrinogen binding.

Regardless of the mechanism of activation, the final common pathway for platelet aggregation is the cross-linking of platelets through fibrinogen. Abciximab is a humanized monoclonal antibody. It is a selective GPIIa-IIIb receptor antagonist.

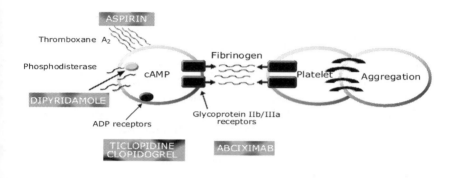

Platelet aggregation factors and antiplatelet sites of action.

3.14   D: Decrease the heart rate and myocardial contractility
The cardiovascular effects of β-adrenoceptor block depend on the amount of sympathetic tone present. The chief cardiac effect results from reduction of the sympathetic drive which includes reduced heart rate (automaticity) and reduced myocardial contractility (rate of rise of pressure in the ventricle). This will lead to reduced cardiac output and an overall fall in oxygen consumption. β-blockers cause a rise in peripheral vascular resistance due to the unopposed α-adrenoceptor effects (vasoconstriction). This last effect has no role in alleviating angina.

3.15   A: Prevents fat absorption from the intestine
Orlistat (*Xenical*) therapy effectively promotes weight loss and improves co-morbidities in obese patients. Orlistat operates by preventing the absorption of fat molecules in the intestinal tract. Approximately 30% of fat that would otherwise have been absorbed passes straight through the bowel and is excreted in the faeces. As a result it can cause 'fatty stools', urgency and increased frequency of defaecation often with anal leakage or oily spotting. These effects encourage people taking the drug to limit fat intake. Orlistat itself is not absorbed, except in very small quantities and thus its side-effects are restricted to the gastrointestinal tract. Patients prescribed orlistat may require concomitant vitamin supplements because of malabsorption of fat-soluble vitamins such as vitamins A, D, K and E. Therefore one would not expect improvement in bone mineral density or increase in the risk of thrombosis. Orlistat is shown to be clinically

efficacious in reducing a person's weight over a period of a year. Study results also showed significant improvement in reducing fasting glucose, total cholesterol, LDL cholesterol and blood pressure.

3.16   E: Inhibits T4 to T3 conversion

Propylthiouracil (PTU) and carbimazole are derivatives of thiourea. Both inhibit the organification of iodine at the thyroid gland as their major mechanism of action. Neither drug affects iodine trapping, nor does either inhibit the release of preformed thyroid hormone. PTU, but not carbimazole, is an inhibitor of T4 to T3 conversion, giving it a modest therapeutic advantage over the latter agent. The quantities of PTU in the breast milk of mothers receiving therapeutic doses of PTU are not great enough to cause impairment of an infant thyroid function. It seems likely that nursing mothers could take PTU at low doses, though the infant could still be at risk for non-thyroid complications of this drug. Significant amounts of carbimazole are secreted in milk, therefore it should not be given to nursing mothers. Thiourea derivatives have several side-effects including a maculopapular rash, hepatocellular damage and vasculitis. The most serious side-effect of both agents is agranulocytosis. Carbimazole is approximately 15 times as potent as PTU.

3.17   A: Doxorubicin

Anthracyclines (doxorubicin) are particularly known to produce cumulative, dose-dependent cardiotoxicity which manifests as impaired left ventricular function and congestive cardiac failure. Cyclophosphamide is an alkylating agent which is metabolised to the active form in the liver. Acrolein, a product, may be responsible for the common side-effect of haemorrhagic cystitis. Chronic liver disease is encountered more with methotrexate therapy. *Cis*-platinum (cisplatin) is a heavy metal compound often used for testicular and ovarian tumours. It causes nephrotoxicity in 30% of patients with damage to distal tubules and collecting ducts leading to persistent magnesium wasting. The most important side-effect of bleomycin is progressive interstitial pulmonary fibrosis with bibasal pulmonary infiltrate seen on chest X-ray. Vincristine is a vinca alkaloid, when used on a weekly basis, there is a risk of progressive peripheral neuropathy. The sensory changes improve far better than motor changes after discontinuation of vincristine.

3.18   E: An insulin sensitizer which decreases peripheral insulin resistance

The thiazolidinediones (TZDs) comprise a major new group of drugs which include rosiglitazone (*Avandia*), and pioglitazone (*Actos*). This group of drugs exerts their effect by activating the peroxisome proliferation-activated receptor-gamma (PPARγ). This nuclear receptor influences the differentiation of fibroblasts into adipocyte and lowers free fatty acid levels. Clinically, its major effect is to decrease peripheral insulin resistance, although at higher doses it may also decrease hepatic glucose production. Although acting at a different site than metformin, both pioglitazone and metformin appear to function as insulin sensitizers and require the presence of insulin for their effects. In contrast to metformin, the effects of pioglitazone may be progressive over time, and its full hypoglycaemic potency may not be achieved until 12 weeks of therapy. Unlike sulphonylureas and repaglinide (benzoic acid derivative), TZDs have no stimulatory effect on insulin secretion. Acarbose acts locally in the small intestine by inhibiting α-glucosidase enzymes; this action slows digestion of ingested carbohydrates, delays glucose absorption, and reduces the increase in postprandial blood glucose.

3.19   B: Doxazosin

Prazosin, terazosin, and doxazosin are peripheral postsynaptic α_1-adrenergic blockers that act on veins and arterioles. Losartan blocks angiotensin II receptors and therefore interferes with the renin-angiotensin system, perhaps more completely than the ACE inhibitors. They do not block the degradation of bradykinin, which perhaps explains why they do not cause a dry irritating cough. Methyldopa, clonidine, guanabenz, and guanfacine reduce sympathetic nervous activity by stimulating the presynaptic α_2-adrenergic receptors in the brain stem. Methyldopa acts primarily on the brain stem vasomotor centre causing the release of false neurotransmitter (α-methylnoradrenaline) which enhances the agonist effect on CNS α_2-adrenoceptors that mediates inhibition of the sympathetic outflow. It results in reduction of peripheral vascular resistance with reduction of blood pressure. Its action on the peripheral adrenergic ending is clinically insignificant and so it does not cause postural hypotension. Minoxidil causes direct relaxation of vascular smooth muscle and acts mainly on arterial resistance rather than on venous capacitance vessels, as evidenced by lack of postural effects. It unfortunately produces significant hypertrichosis and fluid retention and, therefore, is mainly limited to patients with severe hypertension and renal insufficiency.

3.20   B: Dilation of systemic veins

Nitro-glycerine products are both venous capacitance dilators and coronary and systemic artery dilators. Nitro-glycerine products have complex beneficial effects on patients with coronary artery disease. Administration of nitro-glycerine results in the dilation of systemic veins and decrease of myocardial wall tension and oxygen demand. This is accompanied by vasodilation of large and medium-sized coronary arteries with increased coronary blood flow to the subendocardium. Nitro-glycerine reduces the afterload, reduces preload coronary disease ventricular volume, and increases ventricular compliance.

3.21   A: It is an alkylating agent

Cyclosporin is a peptide antibiotic, which is isolated from fungus, and possesses suppressive effects upon cell-mediated and humoral immune responses. It acts primarily on T-helper cells. Unlike other immuno-suppressive agents (such as azathioprine and alkylating agents), cyclosporin lacks clinically significant myelosuppressive activity. It is metabolised in the liver by hepatic cytochrome P450 enzymes. Many drugs compete with cyclosporin metabolism and cause significant increase in its blood concentration (e.g. ketoconazole, calcium blockers, amiodarone and erythromycin). Grapefruit juice also inhibits cyclosporin metabolism. The major side-effects are nephrotoxicity and hypertension, both require regular monitoring. Other side-effects include hirsutism (which is usually reversible after cessation of treatment) and gum hypertrophy.

3.22   C: It has calcium channel blocking properties

Amiodarone has a high iodine content (40% of its weight). It provides the body with approximately 12 times the average daily requirement when given at a dose of 200 mg/day. This means an increased iodine load with possible altered thyroid handling of iodine. With the prospect of hypothyroidism (Wolff-Chaikoff effect) or hyperthyroidism due to increased conversion of iodine to thyroxine. Amiodarone can directly cause both sinus bradycardia and AV block, due primarily to its calcium channel blocking activity. Of great potential concern is the prolongation of the QT intervals due to blockage of the potassium channels. It is used effectively for both ventricular and supraventricular tachyarrhythmias. Corneal micro-deposits occur in most patients receiving long-term amiodarone therapy. This complication is dose dependent and is reversible when the drug is discontinued. The micro-deposits are caused by the secretion of amiodarone by the lacrimal gland; they accumulate on the corneal surface. Amiodarone inhibits cytochrome P450 in the liver thus inhibiting the metabolism of other drugs. This can raise digoxin levels by as much as 100%, as a result, the digoxin dose should be reduced by 50% when commencing amiodarone. Amiodarone might also displace digoxin from its protein binding sites thus increasing its levels in the serum.

3.23   B: Sodium valproate
All anticonvulsants cause adverse effects. The newer anticonvulsants have simpler pharmacokinetics and a reduced potential to cause interactions. Sodium valproate has been associated with the development of PCO, a condition associated with central obesity, hirsutism, irregular periods or secondary amenorrhoea, infertility and insulin resistance. Characteristically there is a low FSH, high LH, high oestradiol and high androgen levels. Occasionally virilism may occur. The underlying defect is not yet established, but there appears to be defective ovarian production of oestradiol, with overproduction of precursor molecules, which are converted into androgens in extra-glandular tissue.

3.24   D: Somatotropin
Octreotide and lanreotide are somatostatin analogues, thereby inhibiting GH secretion. They are indicated for the relief of symptoms associated with neuroendocrine (particularly carcinoid) tumours and acromegaly. Growth hormone-secreting pituitary tumours can expand on this treatment, causing serious complications; therefore patients should be monitored for signs of tumour expansion (e.g. visual field defects). The dopamine agonists, bromocriptine and cabergoline, may also be used, often as adjuncts to ablative therapy of the pituitary tumour. Cabergoline, has actions and uses similar to those of bromocriptine, but its duration of action is longer. Its side-effect profile differs from that of bromocriptine, which means that patients intolerant of bromocriptine may be able to tolerate cabergoline (and vice versa). Somatotropin is actually a synthetic Human Growth Hormone, produced using recombinant DNA technology, and therefore would not be suitable therapy for acromegaly!

3.25   C: 10–30% of the inhaled dose of insulin is absorbed into the circulation

10–30% of the inhaled dose of insulin is absorbed into the circulation, therefore requiring approximately 100 times the dose of subcutaneous insulin to achieve similar glycaemic control. Cigarette smoking increases absorption of inhaled insulin. A bedtime subcutaneus Ultralente insulin injection plus pre-prandial inhaled insulin is required to give similar glucose control to the usual subcutaneous insulin regimens of two to three daily insulin injections. Inhaled insulin peaks at least as rapidly as a fast-acting analogue injected under the skin, and has a longer duration of effect. Studies to date have shown no effect on pulmonary function (i.e. spirometry, lung volumes, diffusion capacity, and oxygen saturation).

3.26   E: Bioavailability immediately following intravenous injection of a drug

Renal failure disturbs virtually every kinetic parameter including gastric absorption, hepatic metabolism of some drugs, protein binding and volume of distribution. The bioavailability of an intravenously administered drug is 100% and does not change in renal failure.

3.27   A: Decline of drug concentration in the plasma from the arterial to the venous side of the kidney

The extraction ratio is a measure of how much drug is extracted from the plasma by the kidney. It determines the clearance (= renal plasma flow x extraction ratio). The time during which the concentration of a drug in the plasma halves is the half-life. The proportion of an orally administered drug reaching the circulation is the bioavailability.

3.28   Cyclosporin

Bartter's syndrome is associated with hypokalaemia due to a number of inherited defects of renal function. Corticosteroids are associated with hypokalaemia due to their mineralocorticoid effects. Liquorice inhibits 11 hydroxysteroid dehydrogenase causing potassium wasting from the distal tubule. Liddle's syndrome is a rare condition of hypokalaemia, hypertension and low aldosterone levels. Some renal transplant patients treated with cyclosporin run serum potassium concentrations in the range 6.0–7.1 mmol/l. This is probably a variant of hyporeninaemic hypo-aldosteronism and is responsive to fludrocortisone.

3.29   C: Haemodialysis

Features of lithium intoxication include thirst, polyuria, diarrhoea, vomiting, and in severe cases, impairment of consciousness, hypertonia and convulsions. Toxicity is usually associated with levels > 1.5 mmol/l. Haemodialysis is the treatment of choice for severe lithium toxicity. In milder cases, symptomatic treatment is usually all that is needed. All patients with lithium poisoning should have measurement of lithium levels and plasma urea, electrolytes and osmolality. Methionine is used as an antidote for paracetamol poisoning, while activated charcoal adsorbs drugs in the gut, and increases removal of drugs from the body by interfering with entero-hepatic and entero-entero circulation of the drug.

3.30   E: Renal function almost always remains normal

Kidneys are usually enlarged in acute interstitial nephritis. Drugs are the most important factors in the aetiology of this condition, which is immune-mediated. Haematuria and renal impairment are usual.

4: DERMATOLOGY: ANSWERS AND EXPLANATIONS

4.1   A: Tuberculosis
Pyoderma gangrenosum is made up of deep, red, necrotic ulcers with undermined, violaceous, oedematous borders. These lesions typically evolve over the lower limbs and are encountered in the following conditions.
IBD: ulcerative colitis and Crohn's disease
Rheumatoid arthritis and Wegener's granuloma
Lymphoma
Myeloproliferative disorders: Myelogenous and myeloblastic leukaemia, myeloma, myeloid metaplasia, PRV, and monoclonal gammopathy. Tuberculosis is associated with lupus vulgaris and erythema induratum. Sulphonamide therapy is not associated with pyoderma gangrenosum.

4.2   A: Nelson's syndrome
Vitiligo is a circumscribed hypomelanosis of progressively enlarging melanotic macules in asymmetric distribution around body orifices and over bony prominences. It is familial in 90% of cases. White hairs are common in the vitiliginous areas. Most patients with vitiligo are healthy, there is increased association with certain autoimmune diseases such as alopecia areata, Addison's disease, thyroid diseases, pernicious anaemia and diabetes mellitus.

4.3   A: Herpes simplex infection
Stevens-Johnson syndrome is an immunological reaction in the skin and mucous membrane characterised by iris skin lesion (erythema multiforme) in the skin and extensive bullae formation in the mouth and conjunctivae. The commonest disease association is with a preceding herpes simplex or *Mycoplasma pneumoniae* infection. Other causes include drug sensitivity (e.g. sulfonamides, penicillins, barbiturate, phenytoin and possibly the contraceptive pill).

4.4   C: Acute intermittent porphyria
Photo-related conditions occur in the typical distribution of light exposed areas, which should make the diagnosis apparent. Thus maximum changes occur over the forehead, malar eminences, bridge of the nose and pinnae of the ears, with sparing of the upper lip (shaded by the nose), periorbital areas, and submental region. The V of the neck, dorsum of the hands and forearm are often involved with a sharp demarcation where clothing and watchbands cover the skin.

Causes include:
1. Drugs: sulfonamide, phenothiazines, chlorothiazide, amiodarone, quinidine and quinine.
2. Immune disorders: lupus (systemic and discoid).
3. Metabolic conditions: porphyria cutanea tarda, erythropoietic proto-porphyria and pellagra (nicotinic acid deficiency) but not acute intermittent porphyria.

4.5   E: Herpes simplex
Koebner phenomenon occurs in certain skin diseases that tend to evolve new skin lesions after traumatic injuries in areas of apparently normal skin. Other causes include psoriasis and warts. Herpes simplex and other skin infections are not associated with this phenomena.

5: ENDOCRINOLOGY AND METABOLIC DISORDERS:ANSWERS AND EXPLANATIONS

5.1   D: Extra-adrenal phaeochromocytomas secrete adrenaline
The adrenal medulla has cells that contain phenylethanolamine-N-methyl-transferase, the enzyme that converts norepinephrine (noradrenaline) to epinephrine (adrenaline), this enzyme is lacking in other sympathetic ganglia. Adrenomedullary phaeochromocytomas, with or without extra-adrenal tumours are the rule in familial phaeochromocytomas.

5.2   E: Bartter's syndrome
Hypertension in association with hypokalaemia is encountered in the following conditions:
- Renovascular disease
- Renin secreting tumours
- Mineralocorticoid and glucocorticoid excess, Cushing's syndrome, Conn's syndrome, congenital adrenal hyperplasia, chronic liquorice ingestion and other adrenal adenomas and carcinomas.
- Liddle's syndrome is a rare autosomal dominant disorder of sodium channels in the collecting tubules, there is a primary increase in sodium reabsorption and in most cases potassium loss.
Hypertension is not a feature of Bartter's syndrome.

5.3   D: Addison's disease
Thiazide, loop diuretics and vomiting causes metabolic alkalosis through reduction of the extracellular volume and hypokalaemia. Mineralo-corticoid excess causes metabolic alkalosis in Conn's syndrome. Addison's disease is usually associated with hyperkalaemia and mild metabolic acidosis. However, if persistent vomiting is a feature, mild metabolic alkalosis may be encountered.

5.4   C: Myxoedema
Galactorrhoea is nonpuerperial expression of milk. Hyperprolactinaemia causes galactorrhoea and amenorrhoea, which may result from a prolactin secreting pituitary tumour or hyperplasia. In acromegaly one-third of patients have mild elevation of prolactin levels resulting in galactorrhoea, amenorrhoea and decreased libido. Similar elevation of prolactin levels occurs in a small percentage of patients with primary hypothyroidism. Sheehan's syndrome is a primary hypopituitarism due to ischaemic necrosis of the pituitary gland caused by postpartum haemorrhage; it is characterised by failure of postpartum lactation and failure to resume normal cyclic menstruation. Turner's syndrome (ovarian dysgenesis) causes primary amenorrhoea with poor development of the breast.

Bromocriptine is a dopaminergic agent that has an inhibitory effect on prolactin and is frequently used to treat hyperprolactinaemia.

5.5   E: Peripheral neuropathy
Exophthalmos is caused by specific antibodies directed to the eye muscles, these are only present in Graves' disease and not in other forms of thyrotoxicosis. Occasionally onycholysis of the 4th and 5th finger of the hand with diffuse swelling and clubbing (acropachy) is observed. Hypokalaemic periodic paralysis characterised by recurrent attacks of flaccid paralysis with low serum potassium is inherited as an autosomal dominant trait. Proximal muscle weakness and myasthenia gravis (like other autoimmune diseases) are recognised associations of thyrotoxicosis but peripheral neuropathy is not a particularly recognised feature.

5.6   D: Medullary cell carcinoma
Idiopathic hypoparathyroidism may be associated with other autoimmune diseases. This type of hypoparathyroidism is called Multiple Endocrine Deficiency Autoimmune Candidiasis (MEDAC). Mucocutanous candidiasis and Addison's disease are commonly associated with this disorder. Di George syndrome is characterised by absence of the parathyroid gland and tetany in the new-born. Functional hypoparathyroidism occurs in patients with severe and prolonged hypomagnesaemia of whatever cause. Magnesium is required for the release of PTH; it also promotes PTH actions on target tissues. Medullary carcinoma and chronic renal failure are associated with hyperparathyroidism.

5.7   C: Surgery can be safely conducted in the second trimester
Transplacental passage of stimulating TSH-receptor auto-antibodies causes fetal and neonatal hyperthyroidism even long after maternal thyrotoxicosis has resolved clinically. Carbimazole and propylthiouracil (PTU) form the mainstay of drug treatment; both cross the placenta and doses therefore should be minimised to avoid fetal hypothyroidism and goitre. Surgery may be performed safely in the second trimester, but is usually reserved for pressure symptoms secondary to goitre or failed medical treatment. Although anti-thyroid drugs may enter breast milk, breast-feeding is permissible when low doses are used.

5.8   D: Sickle cell trait
SIADH can be caused by the following:
- CNS lesions: trauma, tumours, infections, porphyrias and raised intracranial pressure (ICP)
- Pulmonary disorders: tuberculosis, pneumonia and ventilators with positive pressure
- Drugs: vincristine, cyclophosphamide, chlorpropamide
- Malignancy: carcinomas (bronchus, pancreas, bladder), lymphomas and leukaemias, thymomas and mesotheliomas.

Sickle cell trait causes a disorder similar to nephrogenic diabetes insipidus.

5.9   B: 5% will develop type II diabetes mellitus
Gestational diabetes is defined as diabetes mellitus diagnosed for the first time during pregnancy, which remits after pregnancy. It tends to recur in subsequent pregnancy in 40% of cases. Approximately 50% will develop maturity onset diabetes mellitus. There is increased risk of macrosomia and neonatal hypoglycaemia but there is no increased risk for congenital malformation.

5.10   D: Metastatic calcification
Hypophosphataemia leads to depletion of intracellular 2,3 diphosphoglycerate (2,3DPG) and of ATP. The energy metabolism of the cell may become inadequate to maintain the integrity of its membrane and consequently lead to damage or dysfunction of various tissues, examples include:
- RBC haemolysis
- WBC and platelet dysfunction
- Muscle weakness and rhabdomyolysis
- Central nervous system dysfunction and peripheral neuropathy
- Osteomalacia and rickets

Hyperphosphataemia is associated with metastatic calcifications.

5.11   B: Apoprotein CII
Dietary triglycerides in cholesterol are packaged by gastrointestinal epithelial cells into large lipoprotein particles called chylomicrons. After secretion into the intestinal lymph and passage into the general circulation, chylomicrons bind to the enzyme lipoprotein lipase, which is located on endothelial surfaces. This enzyme is activated by a protein contained in the chylomicron, apoprotein CII, liberating free fatty acids and monoglycerides, which then pass through the endothelial cells and enter adipocyte or muscle cells. Therefore, complete inactivation of either

lipoprotein lipase or apoprotein CII as a result of the inheritance of two defective copies of the relevant gene results in an accumulation of chylomicrons (type I lipoprotein elevation) owing to failure of conversion to the chylomicron remnant particle. Patients with familial lipoprotein lipase deficiency usually present in infancy with recurrent attacks of abdominal pain caused by pancreatitis. They also have eruptive xanthomas resulting from triglyceride deposition. Treatment should consist of a low-fat diet that may be supplemented by medium-chain triglycerides, which are not incorporated into chylomicrons. The absence of functional apoprotein CII, with consequent failure to activate lipoprotein lipase, presents with a similar phenotype, although the affected patients are typically detected at a somewhat later age than are patients with familial lipoprotein lipase deficiency.

5.12   E: Vitamin D deficiency
The combination of hypocalcaemia and hypophosphataemia points to the diagnosis of osteomalacia and vitamin D deficiency. Dietary deficiency and malabsorption are common causes of vitamin D deficiency. Primary hyperparathyroidism and hypervitaminosis D are associated with hypercalcaemia rather than hypocalcaemia. Paget's disease is associated with increased risk of fracture and increased serum alkaline phosphatase activity, but the serum calcium is usually within normal limits. Osteoporosis is the most common cause of fracture of neck of femur and is not associated with any specific abnormality in the standard bone biochemistry profile.

5.13   D: Addison's disease
Causes of hypokalaemia include:
*   Inadequate ingestion
*   Excessive renal loss
    Conn's syndrome
    Bartter's syndrome
    Diuretic therapy
    Metabolic alkalosis
    Gentamycin therapy
    Amphotericin therapy
    Renal tubular acidosis
*   Vomiting and diarrhoea

Addison's disease is associated with increased serum potassium concentration.

5.14   B: Primary hyperparathyroidism

Treatment of severe hypercalcaemia (> 3 mmol/l) should be started immediately as the condition is life threatening. The mainstay of therapy is a regimen of hydration, initially with normal saline, plus forced diuresis using frusemide. Corticosteroid (e.g. 300 mg of cortisone or 60 mg prednisolone) given daily are effective in hypercalcaemia of non-parathyroid origin. Treating the primary cause would prevent further recurrence.

5.15   C: Conn's syndrome

Causes of metabolic acidosis include:

1. Bicarbonate loss
    Proximal renal tubular acidosis
    Primary hyperparathyroidism
    Diarrhoeal disorders
    Ureterosigmoidestomy
    Carbonic anhydrase inhibitors

2. Failure of bicarbonate regeneration
    Distal renal tubular acidosis
    Hyporeninemic hypoaldesteronism
    Spironolactone, amiloride

3. Acidifying salts
    Ammonium chloride
    Parenteral hyperalimentation
    Reduced excretion of organic salts
    Renal failure
    Accumulation of organic acids
    Lactic acid
    Ketoacid
    Ingestion of salicylic acid, paraldehyde, methanol, ethylene glycol
Conn's syndrome is associated with metabolic alkalosis.

5.16   D: Peripheral neuropathy
Insulin resistance is defined as a subclinical response to endogenous or exogenous insulin. In the context of diabetes mellitus it manifests as persistent hyperglycaemia despite high doses of insulin. Features suggestive of insulin resistance include acanthosis nigricans, lipodystrophy, hyperandrogenism (polycystic ovary syndrome), hypertension and ischaemic heart disease.
Peripheral neuropathy is a recognised complication of diabetes mellitus and is not related to insulin resistance.

5.17   E: Necrolytic migratory erythema
Glucagonoma syndrome (diabetes mellitus, weight loss and anaemia) is associated with a characteristic skin rash (necrolytic migratory erythema) in 75% of cases. The lesion starts as an indurated erythema at the perineum, face and nose. Within a few days blisters will cover the surface of the skin which then crust and heal leaving hyperpigmented skin. This process takes 7–14 days with lesions developing in one area while others are resolving.

5.18   C: The T-score compares a patient's BMD with the mean value for persons of the same age and sex
Hyperthyroidism and excessive thyroxine treatment are one of the secondary causes of osteoporosis. Plain radiographs are not sensitive enough to diagnose osteoporosis until total bone density has decreased by 30–50%. Results of BMD tests are typically reported as T-scores and Z-scores. The T-score compares a patient's BMD with the mean peak value for young, healthy adults of the same sex. The Z-score compares a patient's BMD with the mean value for persons of the same age and sex. The World Health Organisation has defined osteoporosis as occurring when an individual's bone mineral density (BMD) is 2.5 standard deviations (SD) below the mean peak value in young normal adults. Hyperparathyroidism is another important cause of osteoporosis. It is associated with hypercalcaemia and low serum phosphate level. All bisphosphonates act similarly on bone by binding permanently to mineralised bone surfaces and inhibiting osteoclastic activity thus inhibiting bone resorption so less bone is degraded during the remodelling cycle.

5.19   E: Gigantism

Precocious puberty is defined as the development of sexual maturation before the age of nine in boys (eight in girls) in addition to the development of secondary sexual characteristics. It is accompanied by accelerated skeletal maturation and linear growth with premature closure of the long bone epiphyses resulting in short stature as an adult. It is divided into two types:

1.   True precocious puberty is caused by premature secretion of gonadotropins. Testicular androgens and sperm production are stimulated by gonadotropins and result in viriulization and an increase in testicular size.

Causes include:

- Idiopathic precocious puberty
- CNS lesions affecting the posterior hypothalamus such as craniopharyngiomas, haematomas, hydrocephalus, neurofibromas, tuberous sclerosis, post-encephalitic lesion
- HCG secreting tumours (hepatoblastoma)
- Primary hypothyroidism; it is probably due to direct stimulation of FSH receptors by high serum TSH concentration. Testicular enlargement and other features regress with thyroxine therapy

2.   Precocious pseudopuberty results from secretion of androgens from the adrenal gland or testes. Excessive androgens result in virilization, but sperm production is not stimulated and the testes remain small.

Causes include:

- Adrenocortical hyperfunction (congenital adrenal hyperplasia, virilizing adrenocortical tumour)
- Leydig cell tumour
- McCune-Albright syndrome (hyperpigmentation, polyostotic fibrous dysplasia, multinodular goitre and other glandular hyperfunction)

In gigantism, hypogonadism is frequently present leading to delayed epiphysial closure and thus a more prolonged growth period. Klinefelter's syndrome is the most common cause of primary testicular failure resulting in impairment of both spermatogenesis and testosterone production.

5.20   D: Copper deficiency causes Wilson's disease

Manganese deficiency causes dermatitis and nausea. Copper deficiency causes hypochromic microcytic anaemia while excess copper in the circulation causes Wilson's disease. Zinc deficiency is also associated with poor wound healing. Chromium deficiency also causes glucose intolerance.

5.21   A: Typically occurs in the first week after delivery

Postpartum thyroiditis may occur in 5% of postpartum women, at least three months after delivery and characterised by two phases:

1.   The hyperthyroid phase occurs alone in half of the cases with mild symptoms and may be associated with a small painless goitre. It can be differentiated from Graves' disease by the absence of thyroid stimulating antibodies and a low radioactive iodine uptake.
2.   The hypothyroid phase manifests four to eight months after delivery, which may or may not be preceded by the hyperthyroid phase.

5.22   E: Diabetes mellitus

The risk of coronary heart disease is inversely related to the level of high density lipoprotein (HDL) cholesterol. HDL levels are significantly higher in women than in men at all age levels. Levels are increased by regular exercise (like jogging), oestrogen hormones and consumption of small amounts of alcohol. Levels are reduced by the presence of diabetes mellitus. The major effects of clofibrate are to lower triglyceride and raise HDL levels by 15–20%.

6: GASTROENTEROLOGY: ANSWERS AND EXPLANATIONS

6.1   E: High fibre diet is often prescribed for the treatment of the syndrome

Irritable bowel syndrome is a functional disorder of the alimentary tract characterised by altered bowel function, constipation and diarrhoea with or without abdominal pain, nausea and vomiting, with the absence of significant physical, laboratory and histological findings. Anaemia, occult blood in the stool, weight loss or nocturnal symptoms cannot be attributed to irritable bowel syndrome. High fibre diet is frequently used to improve intestinal motility.

6.2   B: Crypt abscesses

Crohn's disease may involve any segment in the alimentary canal. The distal ileum involvement is characteristic. The inflammatory process involves all layers of the bowel with the formation of non-caseating granuloma, ulcers and fistulas. Discontinuity of the inflammatory process 'skip lesion' across the bowel is also characteristic.

In ulcerative colitis there is diffuse, continuous involvement of the colon with proctitis as an early feature in 90% of cases. The inflammation is confined to the mucosa and lamina propria with crypt abscess formation. Ileal involvement is not a common feature of ulcerative colitis but the distal segment of the ileum can be involved in the inflammatory process from adjacent inflamed colonic segment (backwash ileitis).

6.3   D: Systemic mastocytosis

In the stomach, parietal cell acid secretion is stimulated by one of the three principal mediators:

* Gastrin
* Acetylcholine
* Histamine

Several hormones in the small intestine inhibit gastrin and gastric acid secretion *in vivo*. The resection of the small bowel leads to the removal of the inhibition and gastric acid hypersecretion results. Large bowel resection has no effect on gastric acid secretion. Systemic mastocytosis is associated with high histamine production. In pernicious anaemia, gastrin levels are elevated in the presence of mucosal atrophy in the body of the stomach; acid production is therefore reduced.   Steroid therapy and Cushing's syndrome have been associated with peptic ulcer disease; it has not been demonstrated that this possible relationship is due to gastric acid hypersecretion. VIP inhibits gastric acid secretion, and achlorhydria is a feature of VIP-secreting tumours.

6.4   D: Nosocomial outbreaks

Diarrhoea is common in patients taking antibiotics. Aminoglycosides in general are not known to cause the disorder. It is important to differentiate diarrhoea due to *Clostridium difficile* (which may be life threatening), from less serious self-limited diarrhoea induced by antibiotics. The symptoms vary from infrequent loose motions to severe watery diarrhoea with toxic megacolon. Bloody diarrhoea and abdominal tenderness are not prominent features of pseudomembranous colitis and their presence suggests an alternative diagnosis. The sigmoidoscopy appearance of pseudomembranous colitis is diagnostic but not all patients demonstrate the lesions. As *C. difficile* may be present in the faeces of up to 20% of healthy carriers, the most specific test to determine if *C. difficile* is the cause of diarrhoea is the detection of toxins in faeces. Treatment consists of discontinuing the putative offending antibiotic agent and administering metronidazole, oral rather than intravenous vancomycin or cholestyramine.

6.5   A: Coeliac disease

Jejunal biopsy can be obtained by the blind suction technique (Crosby's capsule) or endoscopically. In coeliac disease there is total villus atrophy with elongated crypts and chronic inflammatory cell infiltration of the lamina propria. These findings are not specific, because they may occasionally be observed in other diseases such as tropical sprue, bacterial overgrowth, lymphoma, and Whipple's disease. However, in Whipple's disease the biopsy demonstrates heavy infiltration of the mucosa by macrophages that stain positive with periodic acid Schiff reagent (PAS). The macrophages are filled with rod-shaped bacilli (*Tropheryma whippelii*).
Endoscopy with biopsy is usually the diagnostic procedure of choice in intestinal lymphoma and eosinophilic gastroenteritis where lymphocytes and eosinophils, respectively, infiltrate the intestine. *Giardia lamblia* flagellates attach to the mucosa of the duodenum and jejunum and cause inflammation and partial villous atrophy. Giardiasis is diagnosed by recognising the cysts in the stool or the flagellate in the jejunal fluid.

6.6   B: The risk of carcinoma is higher if the colitis is confined to the left colon

The overall prevalence of cancer in all patients with ulcerative colitis is 3%–5%. For those with pancolitis and disease duration greater than 10 years, the risk is 10–20 times greater than that of the general population. The prognosis of carcinoma of the colon developing in patients with ulcerative colitis tends to be worse than that developing in the absence of colitis because the diagnosis is often delayed because the symptoms of bleeding and diarrhoea may be attributed initially to a recurrence of colitis. The lesions are often multifocal and display a higher grade of malignancy. Carcinoembryonic antigen is not a reliable screening test for early cases of colonic carcinoma.

6.7   B: Cholera

Protein losing enteropathy is a rare syndrome in which absorption is probably normal, but the intestinal wall is abnormally permeable to large molecules (similar to glomerulus in the nephrotic syndrome) and consequently there is excessive loss of protein from the body into the gut. It occurs in a variety of conditions for example, conditions associated with ulceration of the bowel, lymphatic obstruction, intestinal lymphangiectasia and hypertrophic lesion of the bowel (Ménétrièr's disease). In many cases of malabsorption protein exudes into the lumen (coeliac disease and Whipple's disease). Cholera causes secretory diarrhoea with no protein exudation in the gut lumen. The clinical features are similar to those of nephrotic syndrome and the laboratory findings include low albumin, raised α_2-globulin and a negative test for protein in urine. The diagnosis can be made by measuring the loss of radioactive albumin into the bowel after intravenous injection.

6.8   E: Solitary abscess in the right lobe of the liver

In developed countries, liver abscess (commonly of bacterial origin) usually complicates pre-existing biliary and gastrointestinal tract infections. Pyogenic liver abscess is caused by enteric flora (*E. coli*, *Klebsiella*) and *Staphylococcus aureus*. Unlike amoebic liver abscess the symptoms are those of systemic febrile illness lasting for only days to weeks and multiple abscesses are usually identified on ultrasound examination of the liver. Raised white cell count and other acute phase reactants are common in both conditions. A solitary abscess in the right lobe of the liver is typical of amoebic liver abscess. History of chronic diarrhoea may be elicited in patients with amoebic liver abscess.

6.9   A: Diabetes mellitus

All the disorders mentioned affect the liver. Methyldopa can induce autoimmune haemolytic anaemia and positive ANA. Alcoholic liver disease might be complicated by hypertriglyceridaemia and red cell haemolysis (Zeef's syndrome). *Mycoplasma pneumoniae* promotes cold agglutinin production, which may result in autoimmune haemolytic anaemia.

6.10   B: Carcinoid syndrome can manifest in the absence of liver metastases

Carcinoid tumours arise from enterochromaffin (Kulchitsky) cells that are located predominantly in the gastrointestinal mucosa. They are most commonly found in the appendix or rectum. Clinical carcinoid syndrome is usually associated with carcinoid tumour that has spread to the liver. Tumours in sites such as the lung and the ovary can produce carcinoid syndrome without evident hepatic metastasis. Presumably the liver clears mediators released from the tumour and this clearance is bypassed by liver metastasis or when the tumour does not drain in the portal system. The syndrome is characterised by recurrent episodes of flushing, diarrhoea and hypotension. In longstanding cases right-sided endocardial fibrosis, pulmonary artery stenosis, and tricuspid regurgitation might lead to progressive heart failure. Diagnosis is based upon clinical suspicion and markedly elevated urinary 5-hydroxyindol acetic acid excretion. Chocolate, bananas and tomatoes may cause increased excretion of 5-hydroxyindol acetic acid.

6.11   D: Wilson's disease

Hepatocellular carcinoma usually complicates chronic liver disease secondary to chronic alcoholism or viral hepatitis. Metabolic disorders, which may be complicated by hepatocellular carcinomas, include the following:

*   Haemochromatosis
* α_1-antitrypsin deficiency
*   Hereditary tyrosinosis
*   Glycogen storage disease type 1

6.12   E: Gastrinoma

The clinical picture is that of multiple peptic ulcers and pancreatic tumour. The most likely diagnosis is gastrinoma. Zollinger-Ellison syndrome (gastrinoma) is characterised by severe peptic ulcer disease and gastrin-secreting tumours of the pancreas. These gastrinomas generate high serum gastrin levels, leading to hypersecretion of gastric acid and consequent duodenal and jejunal ulcers. Gastrinoma should be considered in all patients with recurrent or refractory ulcer disease, ulcers associated with gastric hypertrophy, ulcers in the distal duodenum or jejunum, ulcers in association with diarrhoea, kidney stones, hypercalcemia, or pituitary disease, or a strong family history of duodenal ulcer disease or endocrine tumours. Glucagonoma syndrome (diabetes mellitus, weight loss and anaemia) is due to hormone-secreting pancreatic tumour. Peptic ulcer is not a recognised feature of the disorder. Although lymphomas are one of the common tumours of the bowel and may present with mucosal ulceration, the pancreas is not a particularly favourable site for lymphomas.

6.13   D: Hypoparathyroidism
Common causes of acute pancreatitis include alcoholism and biliary tract disease.
Other causes include:
*   Trauma
*   Infections (Coxsackie virus, mumps)
*   Metabolic: hyperlipidaemia, hyperparathyroidism, NOT hypoparathyroidism
*   Drugs: corticosteroids, azathioprine, thiazide, frusemide, phenformin, oral contraceptives and tetracycline
*   SLE, PAN
*   Familial

6.14   E: Ethanol induces hypoglycaemia by direct inhibition of gluconeogenesis
Alanine aminotransferase (ALT) enzyme is more specific for hepatobiliary diseases while aspartate aminotransferase may also be elevated in acute myocardial infarction and various muscle diseases. However, ALT is also present in muscle cells and its levels are often elevated whenever there is muscle damage. The liver produces all circulating proteins except gamma globulins, which are produced by the plasma cells. In the fasting state the oxidative pathway is active to provide an alternative source of energy while in the fed state the esterification pathway is active to store energy as fat. A positive antimitochondrial antibody test does not exclude bile duct obstruction as the cause of obstructive jaundice until other biliary tree tests show no evidence of obstruction.

6.15   D: Hypercholesterolaemia
Fatty liver disease usually reflects excessive accumulation of triglyceride which may be deposited either in large vacuoles that displace the nucleus or in small droplets with a central nucleus. Small fat droplets are usually associated with liver damage, abnormal liver function and carry a poor prognosis when compared with the large vacuolar type.

Causes include:

Large fat globules	Small fat droplets
Obesity	Acute fatty liver of pregnancy
Diabetes mellitus	Reye's syndrome
Malnutrition	Tetracycline
Corticosteroids	Sodium valproate
Ethanol ingestion	Ethanol ingestion

Hypercholesterolaemia is not a condition known to cause fatty liver.

6.16 C: Hyperthyroidism

Intestinal pseudo-obstruction is a syndrome with clinical features akin to mechanical obstruction but for which no obstructive lesion can be identified. It can be primary idiopathic, transmitted as an autosomal dominant trait in which hollow visceral myopathy or autonomic neuropathy might be the underlying cause. Pseudo-obstruction also occurs as a manifestation of other diseases (termed secondary pseudo-obstruction) such as collagen vascular disease (scleroderma, dermato/polymyositis, SLE), amyloidosis, neurological diseases (Parkinson's disease, Chagas' disease), endocrine diseases (hypothyroidism, diabetes mellitus, phaeochromocytoma) and drug effects (phaenothiazine, tricyclic antidepressant, antiparkinsonian drugs). Hyperthyroidism is associated with frequent bowel motions and diarrhoea due to increased bowel transit time.

6.17 D: Cholestasis of pregnancy may recur in subsequent pregnancy

Viral hepatitis in pregnancy, particularly during the third trimester appears to run a more severe course and is associated with an unusually high incidence of fulminant hepatic failure (FHF) with high fetal and maternal mortality. Vertical transmission of hepatitis B virus infection occurs commonly when the mother contracts the disease during the third trimester.

Acute fatty liver develops late in pregnancy, manifests initially by constitutional symptoms often with abdominal pain followed in many instances by hepatic failure with jaundice and encephalitis. The only known treatment is termination of pregnancy. It is not related to alcohol consumption. Cholestasis occurs late in pregnancy, characterised by pruritus, sometimes followed by jaundice, which typically resolves within two weeks of delivery, but frequently recurs in subsequent pregnancies or with administration of contraceptives.

6.18   C: Primary hypothyroidism

The myriad causes of bilateral parotid swelling other than mumps virus include infection with other viruses, such as parainfluenza virus type 3, Coxsackie viruses, and influenza A virus; metabolic diseases, such as diabetes mellitus and uraemia; and drugs, such as phenylbutazone and thiouracil. Other conditions associated with chronic parotid swelling include alcoholic liver disease, sarcoidosis, Sjögren's syndrome, lymphoma and infection with HIV. Suppurative parotitis, usually caused by *Staphylococcus aureus*, is most often unilateral. Unilateral parotid swelling can result from a tumour, cyst, or a ductal obstruction due to stones or strictures. Bilateral parotid swelling is not a feature of primary hypothyroidism

6.19   E: High carbohydrate diet

Common precipitating factors of hepatic encephalopathy include:
* Deterioration in hepatic function
* Drugs: sedatives, diuretics
* Gastrointestinal haemorrhage
* Increased dietary proteins
* Hypokalaemia
* Infection
* Azotaemia

6.20   D: Gastric lymphoma

Consequences of *H. pylori* infection include duodenal and gastric ulcer and their complications such as bleeding and perforation, atrophic gastritis, gastric cancer, and mucosa-associated lymphoid tissue (MALT) lymphoma. Epidemiologic studies have also shown that 95% of low-grade gastric MALT lymphomas are associated with *H. pylori*, and these lymphomas have been shown to arise from B-cell clones at the site of *H. pylori* gastritis. Eradication of *H. pylori* may produce clinical and histological remission of these tumours in 70–80% of cases, but treated patients must be followed closely for residual or recurrent lymphoma.

Patients with a varied group of upper gastrointestinal symptoms that have been termed non-ulcer dyspepsia may or may not be infected with *H. pylori*; at present, there is no generally recognized association of non-ulcer dyspepsia with *H. pylori* infection. Several mechanisms operate in the pathogenesis of reflux oesophagitis but there is no recognised association with *H. pylori* infection. More recently, it has also become evident that individuals without *H. pylori* are at greater risk for gastroesophageal reflux disease and its sequelae, Barrett's oesophagus and adenocarcinoma of the oesophagus. Achalasia of the cardia is a motility disorder leading to failure of relaxation of the lower end of the oesophagus and is not associated with *H. pylori* infection. Coeliac disease is malabsorption syndrome due to gluten sensitivity; it is an autoimmnune disorder and not associated with *H. pylori* infection.

6.21 B: In alcoholic hepatitis the aspartate aminotransferase to alanine aminotransferase (AST/ALT) ratio is 2:1

Alcoholic liver disease is the most common cause of cirrhosis in developed countries. Women are more susceptible to alcohol-related liver disease than men even when consumption is corrected for body weight. Unlike viral hepatitis alcoholic hepatitis is associated with reversed AST/ALT ratio of 2:1. Alcoholic liver diseases include acute alcoholic hepatitis, chronic active hepatitis and alcoholic cirrhosis. Transferrin saturation and serum ferritin are commonly increased in alcoholic liver disease and minor degrees of iron overload are frequent. Alcoholic hepatitis and alcoholic fatty infiltration are reversible with abstinence and adequate nutrition.

6.22 A: Liver abscess

Liver abscess presents with dull non-colicky abdominal pain and fever; jaundice is rare. Jaundice, abdominal colic, fever and rigor (Charcot's triad) are the most common presenting features of cholangitis. Jaundice and weight loss accompanied by palpable distended gall bladder (Courvoisier's sign) are suggestive of obstructive periampullary lesion. In chronic choledocholithiasis the gall bladder is small, fibrosed and not palpable. Parotid enlargement and Dupuytren's contracture with jaundice are features frequently seen in alcoholic cirrhosis.

6.23 D: Intestinal tuberculosis

Certain chronic diseases of the colon predispose to cancer. In particular, long standing ulcerative colitis and, to a lesser extent, Crohn's disease are associated with carcinomatous change. Other causes of chronic inflammation, such as schistosomiasis, amoebic dysentery, and tuberculosis, do not seem to predispose to cancer. Implantation of the ureters into the sigmoid colon predisposes to large bowel neoplasia, but this form of urinary diversion has been largely abandoned. Cholecystectomy may be associated with an increased risk of colorectal cancer, but the evidence is equivocal. Familial adenomatous polyposis (FAP) is inherited as an autosomal dominant condition. Patients with FAP develop hundreds to thousands of colon polyps in adolescence and, if untreated, invariably develop colonic cancer by age 40; it accounts for only 1% of all colorectal cancer.

6.24   B: Chronic pancreatitis

This test distinguishes between malabsorption due to small intestinal diseases and that due to pancreatic exocrine insufficiency. A five hour urinary excretion of 5g or greater is normal following the oral administration of 25 g of D-xylose to a well hydrated subject. Decreased xylose absorption and excretion are found in patients with damage to the proximal small intestine and in bacterial overgrowth in the small intestine (the bacteria catabolises the xylose). Patients with pancreatic steatorrhoea usually have normal xylose absorption. Abnormal results may be encountered in renal failure, the elderly and patients with ascites due to an excretion defect rather than malabsorption.

6.25   E: Oesophageal varices

The liver receives approximately 1500 ml of blood each minute, two-thirds of which is provided by the portal vein. Portal hypertension is present when the wedged hepatic vein pressure is more than 5 mmHg higher than the inferior vena cava pressure. Since the veins in the portal system lack valves, increased resistance to flow at any point between the splanchnic venules and the heart will increase pressure in all vessels on the intestine site of the obstruction. This is manifested clinically by the development of porto-systemic collaterals (oesophageal varices), splenomegaly, and/or ascites. Spider telangiectases, jaundice, hepatomegaly and gynaecomastia are manifestations of abnormal liver cell function.

7: GENETICS: ANSWERS AND EXPLANATIONS

7.1   C: Affects lower limb bones but spares upper limb bones

Achondroplasia is inherited as an autosomal dominant trait. Approximately 80% of cases are new mutations, the mutation affects endochondral ossification. The individual is short in stature with short limbs (upper and lower limbs) but the trunk is of relatively normal length. Complications include hydrocephalus and spinal cord/root compression. Fertility and intelligence are normal.

7.2   B: Gynaecomastia

Klinefelter's syndrome is a chromosomal abnormality with a karyotype of 47, XXY. Less than one-third of patients have gynaecomastia. In all primary hypogonadism the testes is usually small (rarely exceeding 2 cm in length, lower normal limit is 3.5 cm) and firm, this is due to fibrosis and hyalinisation of the seminiferous tubules. In secondary (hypogonadotropic) hypogonadism the testes is small but soft. Other features include azoospermia, testosterone deficiency and elevated gonadotropin levels.

7.3   B: An alternative diagnosis should be considered if chorea occurs with no evidence of Kayser-Fleischer rings

Wilson's disease is an autosomal recessive disease with a prevalence of 1 in 30,000. Its clinical and pathological manifestation results from excessive accumulation of copper in many tissues including the brain, liver, cornea and kidneys. Impaired biliary copper excretion rather than enhanced absorption is the cause of copper accumulation. Neurological manifestations typically appear between the ages of 12 and 30 years and are almost invariably accompanied by the presence of Kayser-Fleischer rings. The amount of copper in the body at birth is normal. Evidence of haemolysis in patients with chronic liver disease represents a clue to the diagnosis of Wilson's disease. The haemolysis is not immune mediated. Asymptomatic siblings that demonstrate biochemical evidence of the disease should receive treatment.

7.4   D: Haemochromatosis

An autosomal dominant trait is one which is manifested in the heterozygote. Persons affected with an autosomal dominant trait are usually found to have an affected parent. If an affected individual marries a normal person, then on average half their children will be similarly affected.

7.5   A: Sickle cell anaemia

Haemolytic anaemia is either congenital or acquired:
Congenital haemolytic anaemia
Membrane defect: hereditary spherocytosis
Enzyme defects: (G6PD) deficiency
Haemoglobin defects: thalassaemia, sickle cell anaemia

Sickle cell anaemia is due to the inheritance of a gene for a structurally abnormal β-globin chain subunit of adult haemoglobin, HbS. The abnormal haemoglobins are caused by amino acid substitutions in their polypeptide chains. The amino acid valine replaces glutamic acid at position 6 of the β-globin chain. β-Thalassaemia is due to failure to synthesise beta chains. Hereditary spherocytosis and G6PD are not disorders of β-globin chain. Methaemoglobin results from NADH-methaemoglobin reductase deficiency which causes the iron atom to be oxidized to the ferric (Fe^{3+}) form, rendering the molecule incapable of binding an oxygen molecule. It causes persistent cyanosis without hypoxia. It does not cause haemolysis.

7.6   B: Leber's optic neuropathy

Prevalence of mitochondrial diseases equals 1:10000 of live-born infants. Mutations of mitochondrial DNA (mtDNA) are their most frequent cause. The diseases often result in encephalomyelopathy, cardiomyopathy, vision disorders, dysacusis and metabolic disorders. Despite numerous studies problems associated with mitochondrial diseases have not been completely solved yet. LHON (Leber's Hereditary Optic Neuropathy) was the first described disease associated with hereditary point mutations in mtDNA. The disease is characterised by subacute loss of binocular vision with a lesion of the central field of vision, improper colour vision and atrophy of optic nerve. Other examples include Kearns-Sayre syndrome which is caused both by deletions and duplications of mtDNA. The onset of disease symptoms is observed before 20 year of age. Short stature, pigmentary retinal degeneration, ophthalmoplegia, ptosis, ataxias, disturbances in conduction in heart muscle, diabetes, and hearing loss occur in the syndrome. The other example is CPEO (Chronic Progressive External Ophthalmoplegia) which may occasionally occur as a result of *de novo* mutation, may be maternally inherited (mt tRNA mutations) or can be of autosomally dominant inheritance. Symptoms of CPEO are ptosis, myopathy, depression, cataract and ketoacidosis.
Alport's syndrome, Noonan's syndrome, Fabry's disease and Marfan's syndrome are diseases caused by mutations in nuclear and not mitochondrial DNA.

7.7   E: Diabetes mellitus is usually insulin dependent

Idiopathic haemochromatosis is caused by an autosomal recessive gene that causes increased iron absorption in the gut. Clinically manifest hypogonadism is usually hypogonadotrophic in origin. Iron deposition in the pituitary gland selectively inhibits gonadotropin production without significant effect on other pituitary hormone secretion. The principal cause of death in such patients relates to liver complications, hepatic failure and portal hypertension and malignant hepatoma in 30% of cases. An additional one-third of patients die of cardiac failure. Iron deposition in renal parenchymal is of no clinical significance.

7.8   C: Half of paternal uncles will be affected

Half of maternal uncles will be affected.

8: HAEMATOLOGY: ANSWERS AND EXPLANATIONS

8.1   A: Philadelphia chromosome
Leukaemoid reaction generally reflects the response of healthy bone marrow to various signals such as inflammation, infection, etc. Abnormally high white cell count can occur in both conditions. However, splenomegaly together with a low alkaline phosphatase score would suggest CML as the likely diagnosis. The most definitive test is a marrow chromosome analysis for the Philadelphia chromosome that is pathognomonic for CML and never occurs in leukaemoid reaction. More recently another useful and definite marker for CML is the presence of *bcr* gene rearrangement on DNA analysis.

8.2   A: Hypersegmented neutrophil in peripheral blood film
Hypersegmented neutrophil in peripheral blood may precede megalo-blastic changes in bone marrow. Many neutrophils have more than four segments; occasionally some have up to 16 segments. It is a very helpful finding and a reliable feature of megaloblastic anaemia.
Giant metamyelocytes may be seen in the buffy coat of the blood, but megaloblasts are seen only in the bone marrow and are diagnostic. Atrophic gastritis and achlorhydria are often present but are non-specific features. Intra- and extramedullary haemolysis occur to a substantial degree in megaloblastic anaemia, this leads to raised LDH. This is an important clue to ongoing haemolysis regardless of the cause. Low reticulocyte count and pancytopenia are features of bone marrow suppression due to any cause. Although these are features of megaloblastic anaemia they are by no means exclusive.

8.3   D: Koilonychia is characteristic and rarely seen in other forms of anaemia
Because of the large iron stores and the availability of iron in the average diet; iron deficiency solely due to poor diet is rare even in females. Gastrointestinal bleeding is by far the most common cause of iron deficiency anaemia and is second only to menstrual loss as a cause in women. Spoon-shaped nails (koilonychia) are characteristic and rarely described in other forms of anaemia. The spleen is slightly enlarged in 10% of cases. Paraesthesia without objective neurological findings can be seen in up to 30%, but rarely progress to cause peripheral neuropathy. Both the percentage and the absolute number of reticulocytes are usually normal.

8.4   B: Monoclonal IgM peak

Waldenström macroglobulinaemia is characterised by proliferation and accumulation of malignant cells with lymphoplasmacytic morphology that secrete IgM. The clinical features include lymphadenopathy, hepato-splenomegaly, and the hyperviscosity syndrome. Bone pain is not a feature of macroglobulinaemia and skeletal X-rays are usually unremarkable. In contrast to multiple myeloma, renal impairment and amyloidosis are quite rare. The other immunoglobulins (IgG, IgD) are commonly reduced.

8.5   B: Haemoglobin A2 levels

Low mean corpuscular volume (MCV) and reduced haematocrit are encountered in both conditions. In thalassaemia trait the peripheral blood smear is grossly abnormal, similarly in severe iron deficiency anaemia (IDA) the smear is markedly abnormal, both show bizarre morphology, target cells and a small number of nucleated red blood cells. Splenomegaly is rare but could be seen in 5–10% of severe iron deficiency anaemia and in 5% of patients with thalassaemia trait. Elevated haemoglobin A2 is encountered in thalassaemia trait, it is typically low in IDA unless the patient has received a recent blood transfusion. Serum iron and ferritin levels are typically low in IDA and high in thalassaemia trait.

8.6   C: Transfusion related acute lung injury (TRALIs)

Leucocytes, have increasingly been recognised as a contributor to if not a cause of, a number of adverse consequences to blood transfusion. The following are the major effects of leucocytes:

Immunologically mediated effect

a.   Febrile nonhaemolytic transfusion reactions (FNHTRs). The typical reaction consists of a chill followed by fever, usually during or within a few hours of the transfusion. Headache and malaise may occur. Alloimmunisation to antigens on leucocytes and platelets is one of the most common causes of FNHTRs

b.   In graft-versus-host disease (GVHD) the recipient does not recognise the donor as foreign; the donor lymphocytes are stimulated by the host's proliferate, and cause GVHD
      Skin rashes, fever, abnormalities of hepatic function, and diarrhoea occur; severe pancytopenia caused by marrow suppression is typical of transfusion-induced GVHD

c.   Alloimmunisation against HLA (platelet destruction)

Infectious disease transmission such as CMV, EBV and HTLV I/II
Reperfusion injury

Transfusion related acute lung injury (TRALI) appears as the sudden development of severe respiratory distress caused by a syndrome of low-pressure pulmonary oedema resembling the adult respiratory distress syndrome (ARDS). These reactions are usually caused by the transfusion of antibodies in donor plasma that are reactive with recipient granulocytes.

8.7   A: Haemolytic anaemia associated with *Mycoplasma pneumoniae*

Therapeutic plasmapheresis is performed using a blood cell separator to extract the patient's plasma, while returning the RBCs in a plasma-replacing fluid (e.g. 5% albumin). Undesired plasma components are removed in this process, and the remainder of the plasma is returned to the patient. A one-volume exchange removes about 66% of such components. Plasmapheresis may be used to supplement immunosuppressive or cytotoxic therapy in initially treating rapidly progressive autoimmune processes. By rapidly removing undesired plasma components (e.g. cold agglutinins, cryoglobulins and anti-glomerular basement membrane antibodies), plasmapheresis provides time for medications to exert their effects. Cold agglutinins are circulating IgM antibodies that may increase in response to certain infections such as *Mycoplasma pneumoniae*, and can induce cold agglutinins mediated autoimmune haemolytic anaemia. Plasmapheresis is very efficient in removing big circulating molecules such as the pentameric IgM rather than the relatively small dimeric IgG molecules. IgG type antibodies are responsible for SLE associated haemolytic anaemia.

8.8   C: Immunoglobulins

Plasma proteins that increase during the acute phase response include:

- C-reactive protein
- Serum amyloid A protein
- Alpha-1-acid glycoprotein, ceruloplasmin
- Alpha-macroglobulin
- Complement components
- Alpha-1-antitrypsin
- Fibrinogen
- Haptoglobin
- Ferritin

8.9 C: Bone marrow examination is essential to confirm the diagnosis

Chronic lymphatic leukaemia (CLL) is characterised by accumulation of small mature lymphocytes in the bone marrow and peripheral blood. The presenting features are persistent lymphocytosis, lymphadenopathy and hepatosplenomegaly. Hypogammaglobulinaemia is often present at the time of the diagnosis. Autoimmune haemolytic anaemia occurs in 25% of cases. The diagnosis is usually confirmed on peripheral blood examination, bone marrow examination is rarely needed. Evolution in to a more aggressive disease such as diffuse large cell lymphoma (Richter's syndrome) can occur.

8.10 E: Autoimmune haemolytic anaemia is a recognised association

Immune thrombocytopenic purpura (ITP) refers to thrombocytopenia occurring in the absence of toxic exposure or other diseases associated with low platelets. The immune mechanism involves IgG-type antibodies. The disease is characterised by normal or increased marrow mega-karyocytes, shortened platelet survival and the absence of splenomegaly. In neonatal ITP, IgG antibodies are passively transferred across the placenta, the infant platelet count may be normal at birth, but decreases within 12–24 hours. It is rarely severe enough to induce bleeding diathesis in the infant. Evan's syndrome is a rare condition where autoimmune haemolytic anaemia and thrombocytopenia occur in the same patient. Leukaemic transformation does not occur in ITP.

8.11 A: Female:male ratio 10:2

In hairy cell leukaemia (HCL) males are affected approximately four times more frequently than females, anaemia and splenomegaly are the most common presenting features. Increased bone marrow reticulin often result in 'dry tap' marrow aspirate despite the presence of hypercellularity, together with peripheral pancytopenia it might lead to erroneous diagnosis of aplastic anaemia. Skin vasculitis (erythema nodosum, cutaneous nodules) occur in as many as one-third of the patients.

8.12   C: Mediastinal lymphadenopathy
Good prognostic signs in ALL include
* FAB L1 type, cALLA
* Young age
* Pre-B phenotype
* Low initial WBC count

Bad prognostic signs include
* FAB L3
* The presence of Philadelphia chromosome
* Central nervous system involvement
* High initial WBC count
* B-, T-cell type

8.13   D: Myxoedema
Hyposplenism is a state, which usually follows surgical removal of the spleen (postsplenectomy). Less often it may be functional where splenic tissue is replaced by abnormal tissue such as sarcoid granuloma, amyloid or myloma protein. Other diseases linked to hyposplenism include coeliac disease, dermatitis herpetiformis, Graves' disease and SLE. Such patients run the same risk of fulminant bacterial infection, as do those who have had their spleen surgically removed.

The condition can often be diagnosed on peripheral blood smear examination. Howell-Jolly and Heinz bodies, nucleated RBCs, siderocytes and acanthocytes are frequently encountered.

8.14   E: Terminal conversion to multiple myeloma
Myelofibrosis is a disease characterised by excessive fibroblast proliferation and collagen deposition in the bone marrow. It is accompanied by myeloid metaplasia and hypertrophy of organs such as the liver, spleen and lymph nodes. It is usually associated with leuco-erythroblastic blood picture, teardrop cells and poikilocytosis.

8.15 C: Factor 8 inhibitors occur in 10% of patients receiving multiple factor 8 transfusion

Petechiae are an extremely important clue in the diagnosis of haemostatic disorder and are only seen in platelet disorders. Haemarthroses are almost pathognomonic of severe haemophilia and often lead to joint damage and deformities. The bleeding in haemophilia is usually confined to soft tissue, muscle and other body compartments. The iron is usually recycled from these sites and iron deficiency anaemia is not a frequent feature of haemophilia. PTT is prolonged, PT and bleeding time are typically normal. Prolonged bleeding time is caused either by thrombocytopenia or by qualitative platelet dysfunction.

8.16 B: Haemolytic-uraemic syndrome

Thrombocytosis is encountered in the following disorders:
- Bleeding and haemolysis
- Inflammation: rheumatoid arthritis and IBD
- Post-splenectomy: surgical or functional (sickle cell disease)
- Myeloproliferative disorders

The haemolytic-uraemic syndrome is characterised by microangiopathic haemolytic anaemia and thrombocytopenia. Thrombocytosis frequently occurs in association with iron deficiency anaemia, the reasons are not clear.

8.17 C: Human parvovirus B19 infection

Aplastic anaemic crises occur more frequently in children with a parvovirus infection, which is characterised by mild fever, dyspnoea on exertion, anorexia, and pallor. Recovery from aplastic crisis typically requires a week, but the patient may need to be transfused with packed erythrocytes until marrow recovery. However, well-known precipitants of vaso-occlusive pain crises (VPC) include cold weather, relative high haemoglobin concentration, dehydration, infection, exercise, dampness, poor diet, hypoxia, acidosis, emotional stress, and fatigue.

8.18 A: They do not bind antithrombin

Both forms of heparin bind and activate antithrombin, accelerating the interaction of antithrombin with activated factor X (factor Xa) by 1000 fold. After subcutaneous injection, LMW heparins are better absorbed and have higher bioavailability. The half-life of subcutaneous LMW heparin (3–6 hours) is 2–4 times that of unfractionated heparin. The risk for bleeding may be less with LMW heparin. Thrombocytopenia is induced by both types of heparin. However, LMW heparin has low affinity for platelet factor 4 and therefore a lower incidence of heparin induced thrombocytopenia.

8.19   B: Pneumococcal pneumonia

Aplastic anaemia refers to a diverse group of potentially severe marrow disorders characterised by pancytopenia and a marrow that is largely devoid of haemopoietic cells which are replaced by a large amount of fat. Causes of aplastic anaemia include

Acquired

Idiopathic

Autoimmune

Drugs (cytotoxic drugs, chloramphenicol, phenytoin, phenothiazines, thiouracil, methicillin)

Toxic chemicals (benzene)

Radiation

Pregnancy

Infections (hepatitis, parvovirus)

Paroxysmal nocturnal haemoglobinuria

Constitutional

Familial or congenital

Fanconi's anaemia

Dyskeratosis congenita

8.20   C: Diagnosis is readily made by assessment of serum ferritin level and liver biopsy

Chronically transfused patients inevitably develop a syndrome of iron overload called transfusional haemosiderosis. Only persons who have received more than 100 units of packed erythrocytes (25 g of iron) develop symptoms of iron overload (similar to those observed in haemochromatosis). Desferrioxamine (*Desferal*) is an effective and safe iron chelator. Pericarditis is the early and most frequent symptom of cardiac involvement. Diagnosis is readily made by assessment of serum ferritin level and liver biopsy. Transfusion haemosiderosis develops more readily in thalassaemia than in aplastic anaemia.

8.21   C: Bronchial carcinoma

Although tumours of almost any origin may present as pyrexia of undetermined origin, some tumours are more likely to be associated with fever. Examples of such neoplasms include Hodgkin's and other lymphomas, hypernephroma, preleukaemia, and atrial myxoma.

8.22   C: Spine
The sites most usually involved in bone metastasis are, in order of frequency, the spine, pelvis, ribs, skull and proximal long bones.

8.23   E: Responsible for neural tube defect in the fetus
Reduced intake is by far the most common cause. Because body folate reserves are small, deficiency develops rapidly (within four months) in persons with an inadequate diet. Impaired utilisation of folate is caused by administration of methotrexate, a powerful inhibitor of dihydrofolate reductase that can deplete folate coenzymes in tissues within hours. Folinic acid rather than folic acid effectively counteracts the action of methotrexate by bypassing the inhibited reductase and is useful in the treatment of toxicity. Bacteria colonising the small intestine utilise vitamin B_{12} and generate folic acid. The lack of neurological findings in patients with megaloblastic anaemia suggests folic rather than B_{12} deficiency. Pregnancy increases requirements for folate. Folic acid supplementation is desirable during pregnancy not only because requirements are increased but also because there is increased risk of abruptio placenta, neural tube defect and spontaneous abortion in the presence of severe folic acid deficiency.

9: INFECTIOUS DISEASES: ANSWERS AND EXPLANATIONS

9.1   A: Q fever
The genus *Chlamydia* contains two species, *C. psittaci* and *C. trachomatis*. The former is a ubiquitous cause of infection in birds and lower mammals with human beings as occasional accidental hosts. It could cause serious pneumonic disease when transmitted to humans. *C. trachomatis* causes ocular infection (trachoma) which is regarded as the commonest cause of blindness in developing countries.

C. trachomatis types L1, L2 and L3 cause procto-colitis and painful enlargement of the inguinal lymph glands (lymphogranuloma venereum). Reiter's syndrome is a disorder of unknown aetiology; it is characterised by a triad of arthritis, conjunctivitis and urethritis. In the post-venereal type both *Chlamydia* and *Mycoplasma* are implicated. Q (Query) fever is caused by *Coxiella burnetii*, a *Rickettsia*–like organism. The clinical features of the illness are protean ranging from subclinical infection to fatal encephalitis and endocarditis.

9.2   C: Fever and transient cerebral disorders are frequently present
HUS is characterised by microangiopathic haemolytic anaemia and renal impairment that usually occur abruptly in children approximately 3–10 days after an episode of gastro-enteritis or viral upper respiratory tract infection. Gastro-enteritis is often associated with verotoxin; only 10% of cases progress to renal failure. *E. coli* is not in the blood at the time of diagnosis. Fever and neurological disorders are very rarely encountered in cases of HUS. The presence of these symptoms is more suggestive of thrombotic thrombocytopenic purpura.

9.3   C: Chloroquine is ineffective in the treatment of *P. falciparum* infection
Most falciparum infection is eliminated in one year; a few persist for up to three years. *P. malariae* infection may persist as an asymptomatic infection for the life of the patient. Chloroquine is very effective in treating all types of malaria including *P. falciparum*, but in certain areas in Asia and Africa *P. falciparum* is chloroquine resistant. Malaria is diagnosed by identifying the parasites on thin and thick blood film examination.

9.4   A: *Staphylococcus epidermidis*
Bacterial infection of a prosthetic joint is a rare, but devastating and costly event. Hip and knee replacements, which account for most of the joint replacement operations performed, have a 1–2% chance of becoming infected over the life of the patient or replacement.

The most common source of infection is seeding from an infected skin lesion especially when infection occurs early in the first 12 weeks (postoperative period). Gram-positive staphylococci comprise 75–90% of the Gram-positive bacteria found in infected prosthetic joints, with *S. epidermidis* being more common than *S. aureus*, in contrast with septic arthritis in natural joints, where *S. aureus* predominates.

9.5 B: Hydatid cyst
Arthropods include lice, bed bugs, flees, mosquitoes, ticks, mites etc.
* Trypanosoma is transmitted by the tsetse flies
* Leishmaniasis is transmitted by sand flies
* Malaria is transmitted by mosquitoes
* Lyme disease is transmitted by ticks
Hydatid disease is transmitted by accidental ingestion of the cyst of the parasite.

9.6 A: Usually caused by *Mycobacterium avium-intracellulare* (MAI)
Multiple drug resistant tuberculosis (MDR-TB) is caused by an isolate of *Mycobacterium tuberculosis*, which is resistant to two, or more of the first line chemotherapeutic agents usually isoniazid and rifampicin. There has been dramatic change in the epidemiology of TB since the description of AIDS in 1981. The changes include an increase in the number of primary TB cases reported and also an increase in MDR-TB cases. Sputum smear is positive for acid-fast bacilli in 70% of patients with MDR-TB compared with 50% of patients with pan-sensitive organisms; this mean MDR-TB is more infectious. Directly observed therapy is defined as observation of the patient by a health provider or other responsible person as the patient ingests anti-TB medication. It is recommended in situations where adherence to treatment regimen is questionable.

9.7 D: Carbamazepine
The clinical picture is consistent with herpes zoster. Prednisolone in combination with antiviral agents has been shown to decrease acute symptoms of herpes zoster. Acyclovir has also been shown to relieve and shorten acute symptoms of herpes zoster as well as shorten the duration of postherpetic neuralgia. Famciclovir, the prodrug of penciclovir, is at least as effective as acyclovir and perhaps more so. One recent study showed two-fold faster resolution of postherpetic neuralgia in famciclovir-treated patients with zoster than in recipients of placebo. Opiates may be necessary to relieve severe pain caused by herpes zoster. Carbamazepine can relieve some forms of postherpetic neuralgia, but the drug is not helpful for relief of acute zoster pain.

9.8   A: Genital herpes
Infectious aetiologies of genital ulcers include herpes simplex virus (HSV), chancroid (*Haemophilus ducreyi*), granuloma inguinale (calymmato-bacterium granulomatis), syphilis (*Treponema pallidum*), HIV-specific ulcers (acute HIV infection or late HIV), and lymphogranuloma venereum (LGV, *Chlamydia trachomatis* serovars L1–3). Non-infectious aetiologies include fixed drug reactions, Behçet's disease, neoplasms, and trauma. It is particularly important to consider these alternative causes if evaluations for the infectious aetiologies do not lead to a diagnosis. Genital ulcers occur in sexually active individuals throughout the world. The relative frequency of each of the infectious aetiologies differs depending on geographic location. The most common causes of genital ulcers in sexually active young adults in the USA are herpes simplex virus (HSV), syphilis, and chancroid. Of these three infections, ulcers due to HSV are the most prevalent, followed by primary syphilis and then chancroid. Infection with each of these organisms is not mutually exclusive, and co-infection with multiple organisms occurs. Genital ulcers caused by HSV are frequently multiple, shallow and tender, while chancroid often presents with deep, undermined and purulent ulcers. When a painless, indurated, clean-based ulcer is present, the diagnosis of syphilis is more likely.
There are a number of laboratory tests that can be used to make an accurate diagnosis. Conventional tests for diagnosing these infections include:
- Gram stain and culture on selective media (for *H. ducreyi*)
- Tzanck preparation, direct fluorescence antibody (DFA), and viral culture (for HSV)
- Serological tests (for syphilis and LGV)
- Darkfield microscopy (for syphilis) not routinely available
- Tissue biopsy (syphilis, granuloma inguinale)

9.9   A: Meningococcal meningitis
Gram staining should always be used in examining CSF, as it permits rapid and accurate identification of the aetiologic agent in approximately 60–90% of cases of bacterial meningitis. *N. meningitidis* is a Gram-negative diplococcus whose adjacent sides are flattened to produce its characteristic biscuit shape. Meningococcal meningitis is caused by *Neisseria meningitidis* (the meningococcus) groups A, B, C, or other serogroups. Meningococci are confined entirely to humans; the natural habitat of these bacteria is the nasopharynx. The organisms are presumably transmitted from person to person through the inhalation of

droplets of infected nasopharyngeal secretions and by direct or indirect oral contact. In non-epidemic periods, the overall rate of nasopharyngeal carriage is approximately 10% but may approach 60–80% in closed populations, such as those at military recruitment camps or schools.

Children younger than 2 years have the highest incidence, with a second peak between ages 15–24 years. In the UK there is currently an increased incidence of meningococcal disease among university students, especially among those in their first term living in catered accommodation.

9.10 A: *Pseudomonas aeruginosa*

Malignant external otitis is an infection of the external auditory canal due to *Pseudomonas aeruginosa*, commonly seen in elderly patients with diabetes. The infection might spread from the outer ear to the soft tissues below the temporal bone and invades the parotid gland, temporo-mandibular joint, masseter muscle, and temporal bone. Necrotising osteitis of the temporal bone develops. The high mortality rate originally reported for the condition (approximately 40%) led to the use of the adjective "malignant" for this form of temporal bone infection.

9.11 E: Hyponatraemia occurs significantly more often in Legionnaires' disease than in other pneumonias

Legionnaires' disease is sometimes overlooked as a possible cause of sporadic, community-acquired pneumonia. Water contaminated with the bacteria is the source of infection, and aspiration is the mode of transmission for most patients. High fever and gastrointestinal symptoms are clinical clues to this disease.

Legionella pneumophila is consistently ranked among the top three or four most common causes of community-acquired pneumonia; *Streptococcus pneumoniae* and *Haemophilus influenzae* are the two most common causes. Predisposing factors for Legionnaires' disease include age > 50 years, cigarette smoking, and excessive alcohol intake. The risk of contracting Legionnaires' disease is unusually high in patients who have chronic lung disease and those who are immunosuppressed. *L. pneumophila* is a Gram-negative rod, it is not readily seen on Gram stains of sputum. The urinary antigen test for *Legionella* species is most useful and should be available in every clinical microbiology laboratory. It is sensitive and highly specific. Results of this test can be available within hours after submission to the laboratory. The treatment of choice is macrolide or quinolone antibiotics.

9.12   B: Specifically used to detect splenic abscess

Indium leucocyte study (^{111}In-labelled leucocyte) is an isotope test where the leucocytes which are tagged or labelled by the tracer *in vitro* are attracted to an inflammatory site. The test is useful for detecting occult abscess and for screening the whole body in the search for a site of infection in patients with pyrexia of undetermined origin. ^{111}In-labelled leucocyte imaging is useful in evaluating the activity of inflammatory bowel disease. Although the scan cannot distinguish between different causes of inflammatory bowel disease, it may be useful in showing the presence, distribution, and extent of disease in a patient who should not have more invasive procedure. Recognition of a splenic abscess may be difficult because labelled leucocytes normally migrate to the spleen. Gallium-67 (^{67}Ga) may be a better choice for spleen study because ^{67}Ga does not normally accumulate in the spleen. For patients with severe leucopenia, donor leucocyte may be necessary as the use of autologous leucocyte might give a false negative result.

9.13   A: The incidence of KS in AIDS has been in progressive decline since the early 90s

While the incidence of Kaposi's sarcoma (KS) as an AIDS-defining event has steadily declined from > 30% in the mid-1980s to < 15% by the mid-1990s, it remains the most common AIDS-related malignancy. With the advent of highly active antiretroviral therapy, the prevalence of KS and other opportunistic infections and malignancies has significantly dropped over the past 2 years. It remains to be determined whether the incidence of KS will increase again as more patients fail antiretroviral therapy. Reports have documented that KS is ten times more common in homosexual and bisexual men than in heterosexual men infected with HIV. AIDS-related KS remains relatively uncommon among heterosexual intravenous drug abusers, women and those acquiring HIV infections through blood products, suggesting a sexually transmitted agent has a causative role. The importance of an altered immune system in the pathogenesis of KS is underscored by its 400 times increased risk in organ transplant patients. As KS is not evenly distributed between all HIV risk groups and is rare among patients with congenital immune deficiencies, it is unlikely that immunosuppression is the sole aetiological factor. Several lines of epidemiological evidence suggest that the agent or agents involved in the pathogenesis of KS are sexually transmitted. Although AIDS-associated KS may involve any organ, mucocutaneous disease is the most common initial manifestation.

9.14   C: Sputum culture is likely to provide diagnostic results for *Pneumocystis carinii*

Epstein-Barr virus (EBV) infection may have a role in producing hairy leukoplakia. Since *Mycobacterium avium-intracellulare* (MAI) occurs so rarely in non-pulmonary tissue in association with any disease other than AIDS, its isolation from a lymph node in a previously healthy individual would strongly suggest the diagnosis of AIDS. Other causes of generalised lymphadenopathy include mononucleosis, toxoplasmosis, cytomegalo-virus, syphilis and AIDS. Serology and lymph node biopsy are recommended for evaluation of patients with generalised lymph-adenopathy.

Pneumocystis carinii derived from human specimens cannot be grown *in vitro*, nor is there a reliable serological test. To establish the diagnosis, the organism must be identified in pulmonary secretions or tissues. Cytomegalovirus infection is present in almost all AIDS patients, it is by far the most common cause of retinitis among AIDS patients. For reasons that are not currently clear, Kaposi's sarcoma is almost never recognised among AIDS patients who are not homosexual or bisexual.

9.15   B: Hypnozoites

It is important to know the malaria life-cycle. Hypnozoites represent the 'dormant ' liver stage of the life-cycle of *Plasmodium vivax* and *P. ovale* infection (i.e. benign malarias), and can cause late relapses after treatment. They are not part of the life-cycle of *P. falciparum*. To eradicate hypnozoites and prevent such relapses, a course of primaquine must be given following chloroquine therapy for *P. vivax* and *P. ovale* infection. Primaquine is not required after quinine therapy for *P. falciparum*, but Fansidar® (pyrimethamine + sulfadoxine) or tetracycline are given to cover the possibility of low-grade quinine resistance.

9.16   B: Measles virus

The history is typical of measles, which has an incubation period of 8–12 days, followed by a 2–6 day prodrome with coryzal symptoms, conjunctivitis, dry cough and fever before the rash appears. Koplik's spots (small red lesions with a bluish white centre on the buccal mucosa opposite the 2nd molar teeth) appear during the prodrome. Rubella has a longer incubation period (12–21 days) than measles and is a milder illness, typically with a low-grade (or absent) fever and no significant respiratory symptoms (apart from coryza). Parvovirus B19 infection typically causes the 'slapped-cheek' appearance, but can mimic rubella. EBV is usually asymptomatic in young children, and mumps does not cause a rash.

9.17   B: Staphylococcus aureus
Important Gram-positive cocci include staphylococci, streptococci and enterococci. Staphylococci typically form clumps and clusters in culture, whereas streptococci characteristically grow in chains of variable length. *Staphylococcus aureus* is coagulase positive, unlike *S. epidermidis*. *Enterobacter spp.* are Gram-negative coliforms – not to be confused with the Gram-positive enterococci, such as *E. faecalis* and *E. faecium*.

9.18   E: Yellow fever
Live vaccines, including rubella, measles, mumps, BCG, yellow fever and oral polio vaccine are contra-indicated in the immunocompromised. The hepatitis (formaldehyde inactivated virus), typhoid Vi (polysaccharide antigen) and tetanus (adsorbed toxoid) vaccines pose no risk, although their efficacy may be reduced in the immunocompromised. Inactivated polio vaccine is available – if needed (not the case here, as less than 10 years since her last booster. Furthermore, polio has also been eradicated in the Americas since 1991). Yellow fever vaccine is therefore the main problem.

9.19   A: Dysphagia
A diagnosis of chronic fatigue syndrome (CFS) requires the presence of unexplained chronic fatigue for more than six months. Although several formal definitions exist, cardinal features of CFS (besides fatigue) include impaired memory or concentration, sore throats, myalgia, arthralgia, headaches, unrefreshing sleep and post-exertion malaise. CFS is a diagnosis of exclusion, which requires the absence of any other underlying organic or psychiatric problem. Dysphagia might reflect an underlying oesophageal cancer, and should be investigated urgently.

9.20   B: Alpha interferon with ribavirin
Combination therapy with subcutaneous alpha-interferon (3 times weekly) and oral ribavirin (daily) would be the most effective regimen of those in the list. Ribavirin alone has little or no effect. Lamivudine is licensed for the treatment of HBV not HCV (it is also used in HIV therapy). New therapies for HCV are rapidly emerging, including pegylated interferons.

10: NEPHROLOGY: ANSWERS AND EXPLANATIONS

10.1   D: Primary membranous glomerulonephritis

Over 90% of patients with post-streptococcal glomerulonephritis have a reduced level of total haemolytic complement or C3 with normal levels of C1q and C4, which suggests alternative pathway activation. Sub-acute bacterial endocarditis associated glomerulonephritis is characterised by activation of both classic and alternative pathways. A similar picture is seen in shunt nephritis. Type 1 mesangiocapillary glomerulonephritis is associated with activation of the classic complement pathway with depression of both C1q and C4. In SLE the classic pathway is activated. Primary membranous glomerulonephritis and IgA nephropathy (Buerger's disease) are seldom associated with low serum complement.

10.2   B: Almost all patients have ascites and are usually jaundiced

Hepatorenal syndrome describes impairment in renal function that develops in patients with serious liver disease where all other causes of renal dysfunction are excluded. The kidneys are of normal histology, the pathogenesis is unknown. There is intense intra-renal vasoconstriction and redistribution of blood flow. Liver disease is usually severe (i.e. jaundice) and almost all patients have ascites. The hallmark is oliguria and progressive decline in renal function. The urine is typically free of protein or any other sediment. Uraemia may develop, which may be treated by dialysis. If liver disease improves, normal renal function returns. The prognosis is poor with over 80% of patients dying during hospitalisation from liver failure or complications of portal hypertension.

10.3   B: Bilateral small kidneys

When a patient presents for the first time with moderate renal impairment, it is very important to identify the duration of renal failure, as it will influence the line of management and prognosis. Anaemia, hypo-calcaemia and dilute urine can be encountered in both acute and chronic renal failure. Acute pulmonary oedema and seizures are a consequence of volume overload in both acute and chronic renal failure. Bilateral small kidneys on imaging and evidence of renal osteodystrophy on plain X-ray reflect a chronic long-standing pathology more suggestive of chronic renal failure. Furthermore, skin pigmentation and peripheral neuropathy are the result of long-standing metabolic abnormality such as chronic renal failure.

10.4   C: Microscopic polyangiitis
Microscopic polyangiitis is the most common cause of the pulmonary-renal syndrome. Approximately 90% of patients have glomerulonephritis. Equally common is renal involvement in Wegener's granulomatosis. 80% of patients will go on to have glomerulonephritis. As compared with the above two vasculitides, the other common vasculitis syndromes involve much less frequent and less severe renal disease. Inflammatory renal artery stenosis with hypertension is encountered in some patients with Takayasu's arteritis.

10.5   E: Vasculitic skin rash is often encountered early in the disease
Goodpasture's syndrome is a disease of young males (6:1 male to female ratio), characterised by a triad of pulmonary haemorrhage, glomerulonephritis and anti-glomerular basement membrane antibodies (anti-GBM) production. There is a characteristic, continuous, linear pattern of IgG deposition along the capillary wall. It usually begins with pulmonary haemorrhage manifest as haemoptysis, dyspnoea and pulmonary alveolar infiltrate by X-ray, and iron deficiency anaemia. The pulmonary symptoms are followed within days to weeks by development of haematuria, proteinuria and rapid loss of renal function. There is no documented specific skin rash.

10.6   A: Low back pain is the most common presenting symptom
Retroperitoneal fibrosis is one of the multifocal fibrosclerotic syndromes, which also includes mediastinal fibrosis, sclerosing cholangitis and Riedel's thyroiditis. The process usually begins over the promontory of the sacrum and extends laterally across the ureters and as high as the second or the third lumbar vertebra. It is more common in males (2:1), peak incidence in the 5th and 6th decades. Low back pain is the most common symptom, which may be accompanied by fever and weight loss. Methysergide a 5HT2-antagonist used to treat migraine headache can cause a similar syndrome. Other drugs such as beta-blockers, (methyldopa, hydralazine) are implicated.
Pizotifen is an antihistamine; its use is not associated with retroperitoneal fibrosis. Systemic diseases associated with retroperitoneal fibrosis include SLE, scleroderma and carcinoid syndrome. Diagnosis is suggested by the finding at IVP of displacement of the ureters toward the midline. The fibrosing process may surround the inferior vena cava, but obstruction of that vessel is uncommon. Thromboembolism and hypertension are recognised complications. The fibrous tissue does not infiltrate the kidneys or the ovaries.

10.7 E: Hyperplasia of the juxtaglomerular apparatus

Bartter's syndrome is a childhood disease inherited as an autosomal recessive trait. The pathophysiology of the disease is thought to be due to impaired loop sodium chloride reabsorption, which causes increased renin and aldosterone secretion with juxtaglomerular hyperplasia. Enhanced sodium chloride delivery to the collecting duct stimulates potassium secretion leading to hypokalaemia. It also causes hydrogen ion secretion resulting in metabolic alkalosis. Accelerated kinin and prostaglandin secretion may account for the vascular unresponsiveness to presser effect. This explains the absence of an increase in blood pressure and oedema despite the elevated levels of renin and aldosterone. Indomethacin inhibits prostaglandin and restores the normal physiological vascular response.

10.8 A: Amyloidosis

Other causes include:
• Stage 1 diabetic nephropathy
• Hydronephrosis
• Acromegaly
• Renal vein thrombosis

10.9 B: Active urinary sediment with RBC casts indicates glomerulonephritis

Henoch-Schönlein purpura (HSP) is recognised as a systemic small vessel vasculitis mainly involving the blood vessels of the skin, GI tract, kidneys, and joints. HSP affects mainly children between the ages of 3–10 years. Males are affected more often (1.5:1) than females and in approximately two-thirds of children an upper respiratory tract infection precedes the onset of HSP by one to three weeks. The hallmark of the disease is the characteristic palpable purpura, which is seen in almost 100% of patients. It is due to inflammation of dermal blood vessels and not thrombocytopenia. Apart from raised circulating IgA the immunology profile including pANCA and anti-glomerular basement membrane antibody test is usually negative. HSP nephritis becomes clinically manifest in only 20–30% of cases. It usually presents as macroscopic haematuria and proteinuria lasting days to weeks. Most glomeruli look normal under light microscopy with only a few showing mesangial proliferation. The most consistent findings are the deposits of IgA in the mesangium. Other cases may show focal and segmental intra-capillary and extra-capillary proliferation with adhesions in small crescents. Granuloma formation is not a feature of HSP.

10.10 C: Sarcoidosis
Clinically apparent primary renal involvement in sarcoidosis is rare, although tubular, glomerular, and renal artery diseases have been reported. More commonly, but still in only 1–2% of all cases, there is a disorder of calcium metabolism with hypercalciuria, with or without hypercalcaemia. If chronic, nephrocalcinosis and nephrolithiasis can result.

10.11 A: Allopurinol
Due to poor solubility in urine and associated dehydration certain drugs can lead to crystal deposition in the tubules and collecting ducts in the kidneys. This will lead to obstruction, which may present as acute renal failure. Acyclovir is rapidly excreted in urine especially after a bolus intravenous therapy. Birefringent needle-shaped crystals can be seen in urine, particularly using polarised light. Sulfadiazine and sulpha-methoxazole which are now being used in higher than usual doses to treat toxoplasmosis in patients with AIDS, can cause crystal deposition in acidic urine. The most common forms of crystals are needle shaped and rosettes. Ingestion of ethylene glycol or rarely high doses of vitamin C results in acute renal failure due to the overproduction and deposition of oxalate crystals. Other drugs include methotrexate and indinavir. Allopurinol possesses the ability to lower serum uric acid levels by inhibiting the conversion of hypoxanthine and xanthine to uric acid. Hypoxanthine and xanthine are water soluble and readily excreted in urine with no tendency for crystal or stone formation.

10.12 E: Fat globules on hyaline cast are often encountered in pyelonephritis
The presence of fat globules on urine microscopy indicates significant proteinuria and probably nephrotic syndrome.

10.13   C: Dysequilibrium syndrome

These symptoms are typical of dysequilibrium syndrome. This is caused by cerebral oedema, resulting from the rapid shifts of uraemic toxins associated with too-rapid haemodialysis in a severely uraemic patient.

The symptoms of air embolism depend on the position of the patient. In a recumbent patient, air foam inside the heart impairs cardiac performance. In an upright position, the cerebral vessels are obstructed, resulting in CNS symptoms. Fortunately, air embolism is extremely uncommon.

Dialysis against a hypotonic dialysate is another extremely rare complication, as modern dialysis machines have on-line monitoring of dialysate conductivity. The features are those of severe intravascular haemolysis, with lumbar pain, hyperkalaemia and cerebral oedema.

Pericardial tamponade most commonly occurs in a patient who has severe uraemia causing pericarditis and impaired coagulation. The heparinisation which is a feature of conventional haemodialysis then causes haemopericardium. This patient would be at risk of haemopericardium, but the clinical features are not typical.

Patients who are receiving rapid ultrafiltration (water removal) are at risk of intravascular volume contraction, manifest by hypotension. The elderly and those on antihypertensive drugs are at greatest risk, and the projected fluid losses in this patient are modest.

10.14   B: Mycophenolate mofetil and nifedipine causing tinnitus

This question should be fairly straightforward. Simvastatin is well known to cause myopathy and rhabdomyolysis, so the potentiation of this effect (rarely) by CyA is not surprising. The interaction between azathioprine and allopurinol is very important, and should be imprinted upon your brain! Erythromycin, as a cytochrome inhibitor, potentiates many drugs. The fluid retaining properties of corticosteroids are well known.

10.15   D: Deletion on short arm of chromosome 11

Wilms' tumour is a disease of childhood, which makes an environmental aetiology (especially smoking!) less likely than genetic factors. There are several syndromes associated with Wilms' tumour, e.g. AGR triad (aniridia, genitourinary, retardation). They are all associated with deletions on the short arm of chromosome 11.

Renal cell carcinoma is associated with cadmium exposure, lead toxicity, and smoking.

Transitional cell carcinomata are associated with smoking, β naphthylamine, Balkan nephropathy, analgesic nephropathy and schistosomiasis.

Wheezing, flushing and diarrhoea may indicate carcinoid syndrome, which is not associated with renal pathology. Nerve deafness, especially if familial, may indicate Alport's syndrome. Asymmetrical pulses are suggestive of widespread atheromatous disease, which may involve the renal arteries.

The café au lait spots and subcutaneous nodules suggest neuro-fibromatosis, which is associated with renal artery stenosis (and also, incidentally, with phaeochromocytoma).

10.16   B: Wheezing, flushing and diarrhoea
The red facial nodules and mental retardation are suggestive of tuberous sclerosis, which is associated with polycystic kidneys (the gene locus is very close to the gene responsible for autosomal dominant polycystic kidney disease). Wheezing, flushing and diarrhoea may indicate carcinoid syndrome, which is not associated with renal pathology.

Nerve deafness, especially if familial, may indicate Alport's syndrome.

Asymmetrical pulses are suggestive of widespread atheromatous disease, which may involve the renal arteries. The café au lait spots and subcutaneous nodules suggest neurofibromatosis, which is associated with renal artery stenosis (and also, incidentally, with phaeochromocytoma).

10.17   E: Renal involvement
The presence, and severity, of renal involvement are indicators of poor prognosis. Older patients tend to fare less well, usually as a result of infective complications of treatment. Alveolar haemorrhage is a poor prognostic sign, as it is the cause of the majority of deaths in patients with the condition. However, presence of extra-renal vasculitis is not thought to be indicative of a poor prognosis; indeed some studies suggest it may place patients into a good prognostic group. Presence of cANCA, although a useful aid to diagnosis, is not a prognostic indicator.

Factors influencing renal   prognosis include proportion of sclerosed glomeruli on renal biopsy, and degree of interstitial scarring and atrophy. However, a high proportion of active crescents is not a prognostic indicator. The initial response to therapy (by 2 weeks) is also a useful prognostic indicator.

10.18   B: Haematuria

- There is reduced renal reabsorption for glucose in pregnancy, which may cause glycosuria. However, patients with persistent glycosuria should be investigated with a glucose tolerance test at around 24 weeks.
- Haematuria is not a feature of normal pregnancy
- Ketonuria may also be seen in normal pregnancy, as a result of the increased metabolic requirements.
- Early in pregnancy, the plasma osmolality falls by an average of 10mOsmol/kg. This is principally due to hyponatraemia. The osmotic thresholds for ADH release are reduced, so that ADH is not suppressed.
- Dilatation of the renal pelvises and ureters is seen in 90% of women by the third trimester.
- Other physiological changes in pregnancy include: increased creatinine clearance; reduction in plasma uric acid (by 25% in 1st trimester); decreased potassium excretion; hypercalcuria; mild proteinuria (up to 500mg/24 hours).

11: NEUROLOGY: ANSWERS AND EXPLANATIONS

11.1   C: Thymoma on computed tomography scan (CT scan) of the chest

Myasthenia gravis is an acquired autoimmune disorder associated with acetylcholine receptor deficiency at the motor endplate. The ocular muscle involvement is usually, bilateral, asymmetrical and typically associated with ptosis and diplopia. Pupillary and accommodation reflexes are characteristically normal. Two-thirds of patients with myasthenia gravis have thymic hyperplasia and 10%–15% will have thymoma. The creatinine phosphokinase (CPK) is typically normal. Exophthalmos and diplopia are suggestive of Graves' disease. There is restriction in upward and/or outward gaze; this is due not to weakness of the superior eye muscles but to swelling and fibrosis of the inferior rectus and inferior oblique muscles beneath the globe.

11.2   A: Double vision on looking upward

Cavernous sinus thrombosis is usually due to a suppurative process in the orbit, nasal sinuses, or upper half of the face usually caused by *Staphylococcus aureus* infection.
The condition is severe with high fever, headache, malaise, nausea, vomiting, and convulsions. Chemosis, oedema and cyanosis of the upper face occur due to obstruction of the ophthalmic vein. Ophthalmoplegia is secondary to damage to the third, fourth, and sixth cranial nerves. Eye pain and hyperaesthesia of the forehead (not the chin) is due to damage to the first division of the trigeminal nerve. Retinal haemorrhage and papilloedema are late events. Visual acuity may be normal or mildly impaired.

11.3   A: The trauma to the head is usually minor and often forgotten by the patient

The clinical syndrome develops weeks and even months after the original trauma. The minor head injury might not be remembered by the patient. Headache is the earliest feature and may be present almost from the time of the injury, subsequently, subtle mental changes may occur such as lethargy, loss of initiative, somnolence and even confusion. If untreated, patients may progress to signs and symptoms of tentorial herniation. The bleeding is from cerebral veins and neck stiffness is a feature of arachnoid matter irritation due to subarachnoid haemorrhage. Lumbar puncture should be avoided because of the potential risk of tentorial herniation

11.4 A: Pia mater
Pain sensitive structures within the central nervous system (CNS) include the following:
* Dura mater
* Cranial nerves V, IX, X
* Blood vessels

Other brain structures are not particularly sensitive to painful stimuli due to the paucity of pain sensitive nerve endings in these structures.

11.5 B: Absent ankle jerk
Vitamin B_{12} deficiency causes degeneration of the white matter in the dorsal and lateral columns of the spinal cord, peripheral nerves, optic nerves and cerebral hemispheres. Multiple sclerosis (MS) is one of the demyelinating diseases where the loss of myelin sheath also occurs primarily in the white matter of the brain, spinal cord and optic nerves. Neurological manifestations of vitamin B_{12} deficiency include a sensory peripheral neuropathy, with absent distal tendon reflexes and distal sensory loss. As the illness progresses, subacute combined degeneration of the cord develops and the patient may develop Babinski's sign and sensory ataxia. Pyramidal signs, cerebellar ataxia and pallor of the optic disc are also common features of MS. Sensory loss consistent with peripheral neuropathy is not a feature of MS. Barber's chair sign is most commonly due to MS but is not diagnostic since it may occur in other lesions of the cervical cord such as cord compression, syringomyelia and vitamin B_{12} deficiency.

11.6 D: Strong familial tendency
Essential tremor manifests as tremor of the hand, head, and least frequently the voice. Compared with Parkinson's tremor, it is more rapid and occurs on volitional movement. It is not associated with rigidity or hypokinesia. It is suppressed by alcohol and beta-blocker drugs. There is strong family history and the incidence distributed as an autosomal dominant trait. Though it manifests in the elderly, the age of onset varies and it can start as mild tremor in the third decade and worsen with advancing age.

11.7 B: Foot drop
The sciatic nerve originates in the sacral plexus mainly from the spinal segment L5 to S2. It supplies muscles that cause extension of the thigh and flexion of the leg. It divides into two major branches, the tibial nerve and the common peroneal nerve, which are responsible for all foot movements. Anterior thigh and medial leg sensory loss is typical of femoral nerve lesion. The femoral nerve mediates flexion of the hip. Sciatica is pain in the distribution of the sciatic nerve regardless of the aetiology.

11.8   B: Lewy bodies

The characteristic microscopic finding in Parkinson's disease is the Lewy body. A cytoplasmic inclusion, the eosinophilic Lewy body typically consists of a dense core surrounded by a less intensely stained region and a faint halo. The peripheral halo of the Lewy body is comprised of neurofilaments that stain for tau and ubiquitin. Lewy bodies have been identified in other disorders (i.e. cortico-basal ganglionic degeneration and diffuse Lewy body disease). In addition, incidental Lewy bodies have been noted during post-mortem examination of elderly patients, with increasing prevalence in patients 60 years of age and older. The significance of this finding is unclear, although a preclinical form of Parkinson's disease has been suggested as the cause.

11.9   B: Haemochromatosis

Chorea refers to brief involuntary, irregular, non-rhythmic, non-repetitive semi-purposeful movement manifested by milkmaid grip, inability to keep the tongue protruded, stuttering gait and clumsiness with dropping objects. Common causes of chorea include:

Hereditary: Huntington's disease, Wilson's disease, ataxia telangiectasia
Infections: Sydenham's chorea, encephalitis
Drugs: levodopa, oestrogen, phenytoin
Metabolic and endocrine: chorea gravidarum, thyrotoxicosis
Vascular: lupus erythematosus, polycythaemia rubra vera (PRV)
Unknown: senile chorea

11.10   E: Myasthenia gravis

Autonomic neuropathy commonly associates with other forms of neuropathy. It can be asymptomatic or cause incapacitating disability.
Three types of dysfunction are prominent:

Gastrointestinal: gastroparesis, episodic nocturnal diarrhoea, and colonic dilatation
Cardiovascular: postural hypotension, elevated heart rate, loss of respiratory sinus arrhythmia
Genitourinary: large residual volume, retrograde ejaculation, and impotence

Causes:
CNS (central nervous system)
Primary selective autonomic failure (Shy-Drager syndrome)
Parkinson's disease
Wernicke's encephalopathy
Syringomyelia/syringobulbia
Peripheral nervous system
Familial dysautonomia (Riley-Day syndrome)
Familial amyloidosis
Guillain-Barré syndrome
Diabetes mellitus
Tabes dorsalis
Alcoholic nutritional neuropathy
Eaton-Lambert syndrome but not in myasthenia gravis

11.11   D: Multiple sclerosis

This patient exhibits multifocal neurological dysfunction involving the optic nerve, cerebellum and spinal cord. The neurological symptoms develop at different times during the period of her illness. The MRI revealed evidence of white matter discrete lesions. The whole picture is highly suggestive of multiple sclerosis. Syringomyelia and amyotrophic lateral sclerosis are not associated with specific brain abnormalities on MRI scan. On the other hand, brain secondary metastases are usually associated with multiple lesions, but often there is prominent interstitial oedema surrounding the lesions with or without tissue or midline shift. Multiple cerebral infarcts often affect the grey and white matter of the brain unlike the pathological process in MS (demyelination) which means lesions are confined exclusively to the white matter where the myelin sheath exists.

11.12   B: Loss of pain and position sense with preservation of touch and temperature

Syringomyelia is a disorder characterised by slowly progressive enlargement of a fluid filled cyst 'syrinx' within the cord or medulla oblongata. It can cause damage to the anterior horn cells, the crossing of the spinothalamic tract fibres and the lateral corticospinal tract at the cervical or thoracic level. The clinical features include muscular weakness in the hand and arms, scoliosis, loss of arm reflexes and spastic weakness with bilateral upgoing toes in the lower extremities. 'Dissociate sensory loss' where there is impaired perception of pain and temperature with preserved light touch and propioception perception in the neck, arm and upper trunk. Extension into the medulla oblongata may cause nystagmus, dysphagia, or wasting of the tongue. Some patients have hydrocephalus or cerebellar signs related to an associated congenital craniocervical malformations (Chiari malformation).

11.13   E: Cluster headache
The features are classical for cluster headache. Cluster headache afflicts less than one in a thousand in the general population. The majority of sufferers are men. The syndrome is characterised by frequent attacks of intense pain localised in and around the eye on one side, characteristically accompanied by conjunctival infection and lacrimation in this eye, along with nasal stuffiness on the same side and sometimes Horner's syndrome. All signs and symptoms are strictly unilateral and occur during attacks lasting between 15 minutes and three hours. The attacks occur from one to eight daily during a period lasting from some weeks to months. After a remission of varying duration, the same pattern recurs. In contrast to migraine, during an attack the cluster patient prefers to pace about. Attacks frequently occur at night. Recent findings suggest a pivotal role of the hypothalamus in relation to the pathophysiology. Sumatriptan injection or oxygen inhalation aborts pain attacks in most patients. The most frequently used prophylactic agents are verapamil, lithium and steroids.

11.14   B: Posterior cerebral artery
Ipsilateral third nerve palsy with contralateral hemiplegia (Weber's syndrome) is caused by interruption of the posterior artery blood supply to the cerebral peduncle and the midbrain tegmentum.

11.15   B: Visual evoked potentials (VEPs)
The clinical picture is highly suggestive of multiple lesions in the central nervous system and spinal cord. Also the presence of transient phenomena in the past (the leg symptoms) makes demyelinating disorders the most likely diagnosis. Visual evoked potentials (VEPs) are averaged cerebral potentials evoked by visual stimuli (a flash or black-and-white checkerboard pattern) and detected by scalp electrodes placed over the occiput. The method is highly sensitive for detecting demyelination of the optic nerve and central visual pathways. In multiple sclerosis, VEPs may demonstrate abnormality when the MRI is normal, because the optic nerves are often involved early and may be asymptomatic.

11.16   C: Bilateral facial nerve palsy occurs in 50% of cases

Multiple sclerosis is a disorder of unknown aetiology, defined by its clinical characters and by typical scattered areas of brain, optic nerve and spinal cord demyelination. It has a remitting and relapsing course. It is almost unknown in oriental people and among African blacks. Migrants from a high to a low prevalence area have a reduced risk of developing the disease. This is true only for those who move before the age of 15 years. Elevation of body temperature by as little as 0.5°C noticeably worsen the neurological deficit in some patients, this is the result of slowed axonal conduction induced by heat. Pregnancy has no ill effect on the course of the disease. Bad prognostic signs include male patients, young patients, incomplete recovery from the initial attack, and recurrent relapses with short recovery periods. Motor, brain stem, and cerebellar dysfunction at the outset of the disease are associated with relatively poor outcome as well. Recently Interferon-alpha has been found to be helpful in selected cases. Facial nerve palsy is not a recognised feature of multiple sclerosis.

11.17   E: Progressive multifocal leucoencephalopathy

Prion diseases are fatal neurological disorders associated with the accumulation within the CNS of insoluble aggregates of modified cell membrane protein called prion protein (PRP). Only four human diseases have been associated with the accumulation of prion protein in the CNS and they include Kuru, Creutzfeldt-Jakob disease, fatal familial insomnia and Gerstmann Sträussler disease.

11.18   A: Myasthenia gravis

Normal CSF gamma globulin is < 13% of total CSF protein, the gamma globulin is mostly IgG, but often contains IgA and IgM. Separate discrete oligoclonal bands in the gamma globulin region are seen in 90% of multiple sclerosis patients. Other conditions associated with a similar CSF finding include: subacute sclerosing panencephalitis (SSPE), chronic meningitis, neurosyphilis, and any condition that causes peripheral paraproteinaemia like multiple myeloma. Myasthenia gravis is a disease of the neuromuscular junction and is not associated with any changes in the CSF.

11.19   A: The pituitary gland is congenitally absent

In this syndrome the sella turcica is enlarged and filled with CSF. The pituitary gland is flattened along the posterior part of the floor. The etiology is unknown, but the syndrome has been postulated to be due to incomplete formation of the diaphragma sella, permitting CSF pressure to be transmitted to the sella and gradually leading to herniation of the arachnoid and remodeling of the sella. Nearly all patients are asymptomatic, though some may have non-specific headache. The syndrome is seen commonly in multiparous obese women and is associated with systemic hypertension and CSF rhinorrhea. Endocrine function is generally normal, though diminished TSH and gonadotrophin secretion may be encountered.

11.20   C: The CSF pressure recording is within normal limit in 50% of cases

Benign intracranial hypertension (BIH) also known as pseudo-tumour cerebri is a syndrome of increased intracranial pressure unaccompanied by localizing neurological signs, intracranial mass lesion, or cerebrospinal fluid (CSF) outflow obstruction in an alert, otherwise healthy looking patient. The causal mechanism is unknown. Although it may present as asymptomatic papilloedema, most patients complain of headache with or without nausea and vomiting. Bilateral papilloedema, the cardinal feature, is almost invariably present and may be associated with haemorrhages, exudates or both. Visual loss, the only serious complication of BIH, may occur early in the course of the disease. The lumbar spinal fluid pressure is usually elevated, frequently above 300 mm CSF, hence the name intracranial hypertension. Diplopia, caused by unilateral or bilateral abducens nerve palsy, may develop as a false localizing sign.
Disorders associated with BIH include the following:
Endocrine: Addison's disease, Cushing's syndrome, obesity, steroid therapy/withdrawal
Drugs: Nalidixic acid, phenytoin, tetracycline, vitamin A
Haematological disorders: cryoglobulinaemia, iron deficiency anaemia.

12: OPHTHALMOLOGY: ANSWERS AND EXPLANATIONS

12.1 B: Swelling of the optic disc on ophthalmoscopic examination of the retina

Optic neuritis is a demyelinating disease of the optic nerve head characterised by acute pain behind the eyes, more on moving the eyes with rapid deterioration of visual acuity and central scotoma. On examination of the retina the changes are difficult to differentiate from papilloedema. Headache and enlargement of the blind spot with normal peripheral field are characteristic of papilloedema. Both conditions can be associated with slurred speech or limb weakness; this is more likely related to the underlying cause. History of recurrent transient arm/leg weakness, cerebellar signs or other deficit is typical of multiple sclerosis that is commonly associated with optic neuritis.

12.2 D: Is a 74-year-old man with multiple cholesterol emboli on fundoscopy

Branch retinal artery occlusion can lead to altitudinal field defect with visual loss in either the upper or the lower visual field. Fundoscopy may demonstrate embolic material within blood vessels. Anterior ischaemic neuropathy due to vasculitis of the posterior ciliary arteries usually causes altitudinal visual loss. A patient who denies the fact that he is blind because he is not aware of the visual loss is a recognised feature of cortical blindness. Macular degeneration is associated with central scotoma and loss of central vision in the affected eye. Swelling of the optic disc due to papilloedema is often associated with tunnel vision. Acromegaly is typically associated with bitemporal hemianopia.

12.3 E: Ocular myaesthenia gravis

The patient has signs attributable to reduced function of the lateral rectus, levator palpebra superioris, inferior rectus and superior oblique. He does however have normal function of the inferior oblique and superior rectus. These signs are not compatible with a single lesion. The superior branch of the third cranial nerve would be expected to affect the levator and the superior rectus. The pupil is not affected and there is subjective variability.

12.4 B: Photophobia on ophthalmoscopy

Conjunctivitis causes a purulent discharge and is irritable but not painful. HLA B27 associated uveitis is associated with ocular injection, photophobia, miosis (due to ciliary spasm), normal or near normal visual acuity and a normal fundus.

13: PSYCHIATRY: ANSWERS AND EXPLANATIONS

13.1   D: Grasp reflex
Somatic complaints such as anorexia, weight loss and headache are features of both conditions, though more prominent in patients with depression. The behavioural and cognitive functions are affected in both conditions. Poor concentration, poor attention span, poor memory and social withdrawal are encountered in both. Grasp reflex and other primitive reflexes indicate neuronal loss in the frontal lobe, which does not occur in depression. A positive response to antidepressant treatment is a reliable sign in favour of depression.

13.2   C: A 50-year-old man with prior suicide attempts
A variety of factors are associated with an increased risk of suicide.
1.   Psychiatric disorder: psychiatric illness is the strongest predictor of suicide. The most common associated psychiatric disorders include depression, alcoholism and personality disorders.
2.   History of previous suicide attempts or threats: patients with a prior history of suicide attempts are 5 to 6 times more likely to make another attempt. Furthermore, up to 50% of successful victims have made a prior attempt.
3.   Age and sex: the risk of suicide increases with increasing age. It is more common in the elderly. Females attempt suicide four times more frequently than males, but males are successful 3 times more often.
4.   Marital status: higher risk occurs among those who have never married, widowed or separated.
Other factors include unemployment, chronic painful conditions, terminally ill patients and those who live alone. HIV infection alone does not appear to increase the risk of suicide.

13.3   D: The disorder may be a sequel of group A β-haemolytic streptococcal pharyngitis
Obsessive-compulsive disorder (OCD) is a common major mental disorder. It is characterised by anxiety-provoking intrusive thoughts and repetitive behaviours. Obsessions may consist of aggressive thoughts and impulses, fears of contamination by germs or dirt. Compulsions such as washing, checking, or counting are rituals whose purpose is to neutralise or reverse the fears. Unlike thought insertion which is one of the cardinal features of schizophrenia, obsessive thoughts are a product of one's mind rather than inserted by anyone or any outside influence, and are perceived as senseless and intrusive into conscious awareness. Feelings of guilt are

suggestive of depression, however, depression can develop secondary to OCD. The thought and acts are not pleasurable and are unpleasantly repetitive. The patient often has unsuccessfully tried to resist them.

One of the most recent developments is the identification of a paediatric subgroup of patients with OCD characterised by prepubertal acute onset after group A β-haemolytic streptococcal pharyngitis. It has been postulated that the basal ganglia is involved in this process, a hypothesis that is supported by neuropsychological and neuroimaging evidence of basal ganglia dysfunction in both OCD and Sydenham's chorea. Treatment of OCD can be difficult because of frequent relapse and incomplete response. Moderate or severe cases require cognitive-behavioural therapy and treatment with drugs. Selective serotonin reuptake inhibitors (SSRIs) are the first-line drug treatment for OCD. Major tranquillizers are effective drugs in schizophrenia but have no place in the treatment of OCD.

13.4   B: Tongue biting

Psychogenic non-epileptic seizures (pseudoseizures) have been linked to stress, anxiety and possible dissociative tendencies. Differentiating pseudoseizures from true epilepsy is difficult. This often results in a misdiagnosis and unnecessary and ineffective treatment. Certain behaviour, such as side-to-side turning of the head, asymmetric and large amplitude shaking movements of the limbs, twitching of all four extremities without loss of consciousness, pelvic thrusting, and screaming or talking during the event, are more commonly associated with psychogenic rather than epileptic seizures. Pseudo-status epilepticus may be more common than true status epilepticus. The patient may be incontinent but never have tongue biting.

Approximately 90% of patients are females, and a 'role model' (a family history of epilepsy or experience of epilepsy in a paramedical occupation) is often present. However, the distinction is sometimes difficult to make on clinical grounds alone.

Prolonged EEG/video recording is the most sensitive tool for differentiating pseudoseizures from epilepsy, but is costly and therefore limited in availability. Measurement of serum prolactin levels may also help to discriminate between organic and psychogenic seizures, since most generalised seizures and many complex-partial seizures are accompanied by rises in serum prolactin (during the immediate 30-min postictal period), whereas psychogenic seizures are not.

13.5   A: Chromosomal analysis

This 18-year-old has fragile X syndrome and the most appropriate investigation is chromosomal analysis for a fragile X study. It is associated in a large proportion of gene carriers with a fragile site on the long arm of the X chromosome (Xq27.3). Fragile X syndrome occurs in 1 in 1,000 male births and 1 in 3,000 is the frequency in the female population who are usually carriers but can express phenotypic features and mental retardation.

Fragile X is the second most common known cause of mental retardation in males.

The phenotype in males is large jaw (prognathism), large low set floppy ears and large testes (macro-orchidism). They also have short stature, hyperflexible joints, ADHD and autistic spectrum disorder.

13.6   C: Abnormal involuntary movements, typically choreoathetoid and usually complex, rapid and stereotyped

The most common presentation of tardive dyskinesia is chewing and pouting movements of the jaw and mouth (orobuccolingual dyskinesia). An early presentation is an inability to keep the tongue protruded from the mouth. A is acute dystonia, which can present as torticollis or an oculogyric crisis with involvement of limb muscles and upturning of the eyes. It occurs immediately or within a few days of treatment unlike tardive dyskinesia which usually occurs at least after 6 months of treatment. Muscular rigidity, tremor and bradykinesia are the parkinsonian side effects occurring acutely following antipsychotic administration and are commonest in older female patients. Tardive dyskinesia may be irreversible.

13.7   E: Ganser's syndrome

Items A–D are all examples of organic brain syndrome as is any of the dementias, organic amnesic syndrome and postencephalitic syndrome. Ganser's syndrome is characterised by:
- Approximate answers (vorbeiredin)
- Somatic conversion
- Pseudohallucination
- Subsequent amnesia
- Clouding of consciousness

13.8   D: Delayed or absent grief

Murray–Parkes (1998) describes abnormal grief as:

- Unexpected grief where the death occurs in a horrifying way & suddenly
- Ambivalent grief where the relationship with the deceased is disharmonious
- Where the grief is chronic though normal in nature. This kind of reaction occurs following a dependant relationship.
- Delayed or absent grief

All the other answers are features of a normal grief reaction as are sadness, weeping, poor sleep, reduced appetite and motor restlessness.

13.9   B: Delirium due to drug withdrawal

The patient in the scenario has the hallmark features of delirium tremens. He has all the features of a delirium or acute organic brain syndrome. There is a fluctuating level of consciousness, global impairment of cognition (perceptual disturbance, disorientation and impaired attention), psychomotor abnormalities (hyper-lert), and an emotional disturbance. The specific diagnosis is suggested by his tremulousness, ataxia and the timing of the onset of the disturbance (approximately 48hours after his last drink). It is also important to remember that between a 1/3 to 1/2 of people with a major mental illness will misuse or be dependent on some form of drug including alcohol.

Drug intoxication and related psychosis is also a possibility as drugs are available in hospital, but less likely given the continual monitoring he received. A head injury is unlikely to present with such an evolution of symptoms, although should be excluded in all patients with alcohol misuse. The neuroleptic malignant syndrome can present with a delirium and autonomic instability and rigidity. Non-organic causes of his symptoms are unlikely given the presence of delirium.

13.10   B: Paranoid schizophrenia

This patient describes several of the so-called first rank symptoms of schizophrenia.

Auditory hallucinations

thoughts being spoken aloud
voices commenting or discussing the individual in the third person (the voices keep saying 'He is so stupid')

Thought disorder
thought withdrawal (' The aliens are draining my thoughts with their rays')
thought insertion (as with this patient)
thought broadcasting ('The neighbours can hear what I'm thinking due to the special transmitter in my head')
Passivity experiences
'made' actions, feelings or impulses ('the aliens made me feel sad and cry by shining the rays of the machine on my head')
Delusional perception
attaching a delusional meaning to a normal precept ('I saw the car and I knew I was the chosen one')

These are not pathognomonic of schizophrenia (they can occur in mania and epileptic psychoses) but when present over a long time make the diagnosis highly likely.
Bipolar affective disorder is suggested by the grandiose flavour to his symptoms. However the behaviour and affect is not that of a manic patient. Drug induced psychoses can rarely give elaborate symptoms (especially stimulants and hallucinogens) but the symptoms would not last 9 months. Cotard's syndrome refers to nihilistic delusions usually found in older depressed patients ('All my insides have died and are disappearing'). An organic schizophreniform disorder is a possibility and must be excluded, but an organic cause is rarely found for patients presenting with a classic symptom profile as described.

13.11   D: Lewy bodies
The patient described has the characteristic features of Lewy body dementia. He has marked extrapyramidal signs, visual hallucinations and variable symptom profile. He is also exquisitely sensitive to the anti-cholinergic side effects of neuroleptics. Lewy bodies are eosinophilic inclusions bodies found within neurones, mainly in the limbic areas.
Neurofibrillary tangles along with senile plaques are the characteristic histopathological findings in Alzheimer's disease. In Alzheimer's there is an early impairment of memory which evolves into more general deficits in concentration and attention. Focal signs tend to appear late.
Multiple infarct dementia classically has a step wise course, with an acute onset and patchy cognitive impairments. Personality is said to be preserved until relatively late in the course of the illness. Pick bodies are agyrophilic inclusion within neurones and are associated with fronto-temporal dementias. Personality change is an early feature in this dementia, but tends to involve disinhibition as might be expected with frontal pathology.

13.12 C: Akathisia

Movement disorders are a common and distressing side effect of anti-psychotic drugs. The most immediate complication is acute dystonic which can arise hours to days after starting medication. This presents as fixed muscle postures with intense spasm. The most classic presentation is of an oculogyric crisis- with the eyes deviated upwards and the head thrown backwards with a gaping mouth. Treatment is with an anticholinergic.

Extra-pyramidal side effects appear days to weeks after onset of medication. There is rigidity, bradykinesia and increased tone, with a festinant gait and mask-like facies. Treatment is again with an anticholinergic or switching to one of the newer atypical antipsychotics (such as risperidone, olanzapine or quetiapine) which are less likely to cause Parkinsonism.

Akathisia is described above and is an intensely unpleasant combination of inner and outer restlessness. Treatment is by reducing the dose of the antipsychotic, switching to a newer agent or with propranolol or a benzodiazepine. Anticholinergics do not help.

Tardive dyskinesia presents with orofacial dyskinesia with lip smacking, tongue protrusion and choreoathetoid movements of the head, neck and trunk. It appears months to years after starting medication. Treatment includes reducing all antipsychotic medication if possible or switching to clozapine (an atypical antipsychotic). It is often mistaken for a worsening of the underlying psychotic illness with a disastrous increase in the dose of antipsychotic medication.

Tardive dystonia presents with dystonic posturing and is characterised by its late onset months to years after starting medication.

14: RESPIRATORY MEDICINE: ANSWERS AND EXPLANATIONS

14.1   A: The PaO$_2$ at its best is not > 50 mmHg (7 kpascal)
Persistent cyanosis without hypoxia (normal PaO$_2$) suggests a diagnosis of methaemoglobinaemia, or sulfhaemoglobinaemia. In a cyanosed patient the amount of reduced haemoglobin in the blood is at least 5 g/dl or more. The blue colour of the skin and mucous membrane is due to hypoxia and not hypercapnia. Hypoxia should be corrected by oxygen therapy.

14.2   C: Chest pain worse on deep breathing and respiratory rate of 26/min
The clinical features of pulmonary embolism (PE) can be diverse and confusing and range from no symptoms to sudden death. Sudden shortness of breath, pleuritic chest pain with haemoptysis and tachypnoea are the commonest features. However, a diagnosis that rests on clinical grounds alone is often incorrect. Several features point away from the diagnosis of PE and include positive features of chest infections such as swinging temperature (>39°C) for more than a few days associated with cough and purulent sputum. Recurrent chest pain in the same location is unusual for PE and it indicates an underlying diseased lung such as bronchiectasis with recurrent chest infection. Haemoptysis in PE is described as blood tinged, blood streaked or pure blood. It is rarely more than 5 ml or massive and seldom lasts more than a few days. A normal chest radiograph is uncommon in acute PE, but the usual finding is not specific. Chest pain on lying flat is characteristic of pericarditis.

14.3   A: Asthma
The diffusion of CO from the alveoli to the pulmonary blood is governed by the integrity of the alveolar membrane, the capillary blood volume, or both (air-blood barrier). A reduction in the diffusion capacity of CO is encountered in conditions affecting the capillary bed size such as pulmonary emboli and pulmonary vasculitis, or conditions that cause changes in the characteristics of the alveolar membrane which include diseases in which some form of intra-alveolar filling process has occurred and the air to blood diffusion pathway is actually lengthened (pneumonia, pulmonary oedema, alveolar proteinosis). Similarly, TLCO is reduced in patients with infiltrative disorders of the lung that affects both the capillary bed size and the alveolar membrane integrity such as sarcoidosis, interstitial lung diseases, or collagen vascular diseases. Removal or destruction of lung tissue, such as surgery or emphysema decreases both membrane and blood volume components and produces low TLCO. An increase in TLCO results occasionally from an increase in capillary blood

volume secondary to haemodynamic changes in pulmonary circulation; an increase in pulmonary arterial or left arterial pressures, as in congestive heart failure, or an increase in pulmonary blood flow, as in arterial septal defect. The TLCO is sometimes increased in patients with bronchial asthma during an attack, but the cause of this change is not known. Alveolar haemorrhage from any cause can result in a false increase of TLCO despite the presence of an underlying diffusion defect.

14.4   A: Female gender
The cardinal manifestation of obstructive sleep apnoea syndrome (SAS) is snoring during sleep and severe daytime sleepiness. Other symptoms include night sweats, personality change, morning confusion and headache. Patients are described as middle aged obese males with wide neck and structurally abnormal airways. There is increasing prevalence of systemic hypertension. There may be increased risk for pulmonary hypertension and cardiac arrhythmias.

14.5   C: Auscultation of the lungs usually reveals no abnormality
Pneumocystis carinii pneumonia (PCP) is a pulmonary disease characterised by dyspnoea, tachypnoea and hypoxaemia that occur in patients deficient in immunoglobulin G and M, and patients deficient in cellular mediated immunity. The vast majority of adult patients have AIDS, however, it can also occur in those who received chemotherapy for haematological malignant disease or organ transplant. It can also occur in malnourished or premature infants. On examination patients usually show signs of respiratory distress (tachypnoea, dyspnoea). Auscultation of the lung usually reveals no abnormalities. The trophozoite does not enter the blood, the organism is identified in pulmonary secretions obtained by bronchopulmonary lavage or lung biopsy and stained by methenamine silver or Gismo stain. Pentamidine isethionate or cotrimoxazole is the recommended treatment (metronidazole is not effective in the treatment of PCP).

14.6   B: Pancreatic insufficiency is almost always identified in adult patients
Cystic fibrosis (CF) is an autosomal recessive disease affecting both eccrine and exocrine gland function, characterised by elevated levels of sodium and chloride in the sweat. It is caused by abnormal viscid secretions from mucous glands leading to chronic pulmonary disease and pancreatic insufficiency, which will be evident in more than 95% of adult cases. Recurrent chest infections are usually caused by *Pseudomonas aeruginosa*

and *Staphylococcus aureus. Pseudomonas cepacia* occurs in 5–10% of cases. The carrier rate is 5% in the Caucasian population, heterozygotes are clinically normal.

14.7   B: Complete remission without any specific treatment

Acute sarcoidosis includes the complex of erythema nodosum and X-ray findings of bilateral hilar adenopathy, often accompanied by joint symptoms, including arthritis at the ankles, knees, wrists, or elbows. Spontaneous remission occurs in nearly two-thirds of patients with acute sarcoidosis, while 10–30% develop a chronic course. Remissions often occur within the first six months after diagnosis. NSAIDs are very useful for musculoskeletal symptom control.

14.8   B: Hyponatraemia

Small cell (oat cell) bronchial carcinoma is frequently associated with ectopic hormone production. The syndrome of inappropriate anti-diuretic hormone secretion (SIADH) causes hyponatraemia. By the time the diagnosis has been made the tumour is usually disseminated, so that surgery is seldom considered. Unlike mesothelioma a history of asbestos exposure is seldom obtained. The prognosis is very poor and survival beyond two years is exceptional.

14.9   E: Inhaled steroids bring acute attacks under control within
60–90 minutes

The mechanism includes both inhalation of cold air and an increase in the osmolarity of the lining fluid causing mediator release as well as stimulating vagal efferent pathways. It is more common in children than in adults. Cromolyn or beta-agonists may blunt or prevent symptoms when given by inhalation before exercise. Inhaled steroids are ineffective.
Inhaled pollens are antigens that can induce a bronchospasm in any type of asthma and are not more common in exercise-induced asthma.

14.10   E: Fibrosing alveolitis

Eosinophilic lung diseases are a heterogeneous group of disorders which are characterised by the presence of pulmonary symptoms or an abnormal chest X-ray accompanied by inflammatory cell infiltrate in the airways and/or lung parenchyma which contain a large number of eosinophils. Many of these disorders are associated with peripheral eosinophilia. The following list is just an example:

* Drugs and toxins (nitrofurantoin, L-tryptophan, sulphonamides)
* Helminthic infection (Löeffler's syndrome, larva migran)

- Acute and chronic eosinophilic pneumonia (primary)
- Churg-Strauss syndrome
- Allergic bronchopulmonary aspergillosis
- Hypereosinophilic syndrome

14.11   D: A positive tuberculin test in a patient with chronic sarcoidosis is suggestive of concomitant tuberculosis

Sarcoidosis is a systemic disorder of unknown cause that is characterised by its pathological hallmark, the noncaseating granuloma primarily affecting the respiratory tract, skin, eye, heart, kidneys and liver. Pleural disease is relatively infrequent, with effusions occurring in fewer than 5% of patients. Clubbing of the fingers is not a recognised feature of sarcoidosis. Although liver biopsy reveals granulomatous involvement in 40–70% of patients, clinically significant hepatic disease is rare. A tuberculin test is usually negative in chronic sarcoidosis, however, most sarcoidosis patients who develop tuberculosis become tuberculin-positive. Hypercalcaemia, a potentially important complication of sarcoidosis, occurs in fewer than 10% of patients and is thought to be due to elevated levels of 1,25-dihydroxyvitamin D (calcitriol), which is produced by macrophages within the granulomas. High-dose glucocorticoids are very helpful in vitamin D intoxication, granulomatous diseases such as sarcoidosis, and haematologic malignancies known or likely to be glucocorticoid-responsive.

14.12   D: The diagnosis of pulmonary embolism is of higher probability when there is single sub-segmental mismatch

Ventilation/perfusion imaging is most valuable in patients suspected of having pulmonary embolism who have a normal chest X-ray. Two or more segmental perfusion defects, which are associated with normal regional ventilation (mismatch) have a high probability of representing pulmonary embolism, where perfusion defects that are associated with a ventilatory abnormality of comparable size (match) are more likely to reflect a regional hypoperfusion secondary to airway disease. Mismatch in perfusion and ventilation can also be caused by old pulmonary embolism, vasculitis, previous irradiation therapy, A/V malformation, congenital pulmonary artery lesion and compression or invasion of pulmonary vessels by hilar or mediastinal masses. The sensitivity of perfusion imaging is high; thus a normal perfusion study effectively excludes pulmonary embolism.

14.13   D: Multiple petechiae in both axillae
The appearance of showers of petechiae over the axillae or upper half of the body is characteristic of fat embolism syndrome occurring in a patient with recent traumatic fracture.

14.14   A: *Streptococcus pneumoniae*
Community acquired pneumonia is contracted in the community rather than in hospital. In the northern hemisphere, community acquired pneumonia affects approximately 12/1000 people per year, particularly during winter and at the extremes of age (incidence: < 1 year old 30–50/1000 per year; 71–85 years 50/1000 per year). Over 100 microorganisms have been implicated, but most cases are caused by *Streptococcus pneumoniae*. Smoking is probably an important risk factor.

14.15   D: In pulmonary venous congestion it occurs immediately after sleep
Dyspnoea in a patient with diaphragmatic paralysis occurs immediately following lying down. This occurs because the abdominal contents displace the flaccid diaphragm upward into the thorax. The onset of shortness of breath 2–3 hours after the onset of sleep is characteristic of paroxysmal nocturnal dyspnoea from increased left atrial pressure. In dyspnoea from almost any organic cause, it is unlikely that the symptoms will improve or remain unchanged during exercise. Dyspnoea occurring 10 minutes after cessation of exercise is characteristic of exercise-induced bronchospasm. The offending antigen in hypersensitivity pneumonitis induces an Arthus-like reaction that requires 6–8 hours to develop after the exposure and dyspnoea may not occur until late afternoon. Typically the symptoms improve at the weekend, as there is no further exposure to the antigen.

14.16   E: Glucose-6-phosphate dehydrogenase deficiency
It is clear that this patient suffers with familial bronchiectasis. Congenital diseases that either cause structural damage in the lung or impair immunity can cause bronchiectasis. Glucose-6-phosphate dehydrogenase deficiency is an X-linked recessive disorder, associated with red cell haemolysis on exposure to certain food substances or drugs.

14.17   E: Low sensitivity for detecting pulmonary emboli in subsegmental pulmonary arteries

The development of fast scanning techniques with helical (spiral) CT scanners has facilitated the use of this tool in the diagnosis of acute and chronic PE. Spiral CT scanning allows imaging of the entire chest with use of intravenous contrast enhancement during a single breath-hold. The majority of studies performed to date have shown CT angiography to be an accurate non-invasive tool in the diagnosis of PE at the main, lobar and segmental pulmonary artery levels. However, CT angiography is less accurate in imaging peripheral emboli in the sub-segmental arteries. The sensitivity and specificity is generally regarded as being comparable to that of standard pulmonary angiography. Technical factors may cause approximately 5–10% of CT angiography to be non-diagnostic. However, this latter figure matches that of standard pulmonary angiography.

14.18   D: Cephalosporin + aminglycoside

This patient has a hospital acquired pneumonia, the third most common hospital acquired infection after UTIs and wound infections. As they occur in hospital the pathogens involved are very different from those that cause community acquired pneumonia. Gram-negative organisms are far more common due to:

A: Colonisation of the oropharynx by Gram-negative bacilli is very common in hospitalised patients – who have often been on broad spectrum antibiotics already

B: Increased risk of micro-aspiration of nasopharyngeal secretions

C: Patients in hospital often have decreased immune systems

Thus antibiotics that will cover such organisms should be instituted, most commonly as a combination therapy. A third generation cephalosporin with an aminoglycoside is the present BTS recommendation.

14.19   A: FEV$_1$ 60   FVC 65   ratio 90% Va 60 KCO 60

CFA typically has a restrictive lung function pattern. Due to the underlying parenchymal fibrosis these patient's lungs have very poor compliance, though high elastic recoil. Static lung volumes therefore a very low. Both FEV$_1$ and FVC are reduced below predicted values, but because of this high elastic recoil most forced expiratory volume will be expelled in the first second compared to full forced expiration – this leading to a relatively high FER (FEV$_1$/FVC ratio). Thus using this you can discount items 3 and 4.

The DLCO, which is simply the product of Va x KCO, is used to monitor disease progression and response to treatment in fibrosing lung disease. In lung fibrosis the DLCO is low, typically as a product of both low Va and KCO, as compared to the occurrence in lung haemorrhage where a low DLCO is a product of a very low Va but a high KCO vs the pattern in pulmonary vasculitis with a low KCO but often normal Va.

14.20   B: Mandibular advancement splinting
Obstructive sleep apnoea is caused by loss of upper airway/pharyngeal muscle tone during REM sleep which leads to airway obstruction and consequent apnoeic episodes. It effects 1–2% of middle aged men. Good first line treatments in most patients are simple measures, such as weight loss and alcohol avoidance. Surgery is really a last ditch attempt to solve the problem. Many trials have looked at the effectiveness of both mandibular advancement splints (a tailor made mouth piece which helps to keep the jaw forward and aids upper airway muscle tone when asleep) and CPAP, seeming to be comparable. LTOT is really only an adjunct in patients who have other co-existent lung pathologies.

15: RHEUMATOLOGY AND IMMUNOLOGY: ANSWERS AND EXPLANATIONS

15.1 D: Acute retention of urine

Inflammatory demyelinating polyradiculo-neuropathy often affects proximal rather than distal limb musculature. The most striking findings on examination are diffuse weakness and widespread loss of reflexes. CSF protein peaks in the second or third week of the illness. Nerve conduction study typically shows gross reduction in conduction velocities consistent with segmental demyelination. CSF cells and serum creatinine kinase are typically within normal limits. Acute retention of urine is rarely encountered with Guillian-Barré syndrome. Acute retention of urine and rapidly progressive limb weakness is more suggestive of transverse myelitis.

15.2 D: Low absolute B-lymphocytes count

Lymphopenia often follows HIV infection. It is generally due to an absolute decrease in the number of helper-inducer subsets of T-lymphocyte, which express the T4 surface antigen. The lymphocytes are also defective in response to soluble antigen and to mitogenic substances such as phytohaemagglutinin and concanavalin A. Natural killer (NK) cells are decreased in number and show functional impairment. HIV infected patients show polyclonal hypergammaglobulinaemia; levels of all immunoglobulin classes are elevated. The number of B-lymphocytes appears to be normal but the number of plasma cells is higher than normal.

15.3 A: The vaccine contains live attenuated human *Mycobacterium tuberculosis*

The vaccine contains live attenuated *Mycobacterium bovis*. Immunity usually lasts between 5–10 years. The side-effects of the vaccine include infection at the injection site and regional lymphadenopathy. Most developing countries give the vaccine to all new-born babies unless there is a contraindication. After vaccination the tuberculin test evidently becomes positive.

15.4 D: C1 esterase inhibitor (C1INH)

Angioedema, characterised by non-pitting, erythematous swelling of soft tissues, can be hereditary or acquired. Hereditary angioedema (HAE) is an autosomal dominant disease due to mutations at C1 inhibitor gene. The defective gene does not produce sufficient levels of C1 inhibitor in plasma which leads to auto-activation of C1 and consumption of C2 and C4. It is further classified into type I (lower production of C1 inhibitor proteins) and type II (functional defect of C1 inhibitor with normal plasma levels). Acquired angioedema may be a manifestation of urticaria; it has recently been described with drugs such as angiotensin converting enzyme (ACE) inhibitors. Hereditary angioedema is characterised by recurrent self-limited attacks involving the skin, subcutaneous tissue, upper respiratory tract, or GI tract. Attacks may last from several hours to 2–3 days. GI or upper respiratory tract attacks may be precipitated by local trauma (e.g. dental procedures, tonsillectomy). Hereditary angioedema is characterised by low levels of C1 esterase inhibitor (C1INH) or elevated levels of dysfunctional C1 esterase inhibitor, as detected by an immune assay. Between attacks, low levels of C4 are noted.

15.5   D: Monoclonal gammopathies of undetermined significance (MGUS)

The incidence of monoclonal gammopathies of undetermined significance (MGUS) increases with age, from 1% of persons aged 25 years to 4% of patients > 70 years.

Many cases are seemingly benign. However, up to 25% progress to a B-cell malignancy or myeloma, which may not become clinically apparent until after 20 years. The course is impossible to predict.

Laboratory evaluation usually shows low M-protein levels in serum (< 3 g/dl) or urine (< 300 mg/24 hours) that are stable over time, normal levels of other serum immunoglobulins, and no lytic bone lesions or Bence-Jones proteinuria; bone marrow shows only mild plasmacytosis. No treatment is recommended. Patients should be observed for clinical and immuno-chemical changes every 4–6 months. The small M-band, absent lytic lesions and negative Bence-Jones proteinuria would probably exclude multiple myeloma as a possible diagnosis in a fit elderly man. The diagnosis of Waldenström's macroglobulinaemia is established by demonstrating a typical M spike on serum protein electrophoresis that proves to be IgM by immunoelectrophoresis or immunofixation.

Similar blood abnormalities are also associated with rheumatoid arthritis and carcinoma of the prostate. In these circumstances, serum M components may represent unusual antibody responses to protracted antigenic stimuli. However, the clinical features in this case are not suggestive of any of these conditions.

15.6 C: A rise in plasma viscosity (PV) is primarily due to an increase in haematocrit concentration

Fibrinogen, an acute phase protein, contributes >90% of PV due to its high molecular weight and marked asymmetry. During an acute pathological process, a rise in PV is primarily due to an increase in plasma fibrinogen levels. In chronic organic disease, the increase in PV is caused by persistent elevation of fibrinogen and serum globulins with an associated fall in albumin level in plasma.

15.7 D: Wegener's granulomatosis

Wegener's granulomatosis is a primary small vessels vasculitis which involves the kidneys and causes glomerulonephritis with crescent formation. It is distinguished from other causes of glomerulonephritis by the absence of immune deposits on immunohistochemical analysis.

15.8 B: The liver clears IgM-sensitised erythrocytes

Class II (MHC) antigens are crucial to antigen recognition and presentation and are found on the B-lymphocytes, monocyte-macrophages, and activated T-lymphocytes. IgG-sensitised erythrocytes are cleared by the spleen while the IgM-sensitised erythrocytes are cleared by the liver. C5a causes the release of non-IgE dependent mediators from mast cells, to increase vascular permeability and to induce smooth muscle contraction. C3b, not C5a is the complement fragment that activates the alternative pathway. Paroxysmal nocturnal haemoglobinuria is a clonal abnormality in erythrocytes, which make them more susceptible to complement lytic attack, leading to intravascular haemolysis.

15.9 D: Cold intolerance

Cryoglobulins are immunoglobulins that precipitate in the cold and dissolve on rewarming. Three different types of cryoglobulins have been described. The cryoglobulins in type II essential mixed cryoglobulinaemia (EMC) contain both a polyclonal IgG and a monoclonal IgM rheumatoid factor directed against the IgG. Palpable purpura occur in the great majority of patients with mixed essential cryoglobulinaemia and are an important clue to the diagnosis. Glomerulonephritis occurs in a substantial minority and is a major cause of death. Cold intolerance are more likely to be a feature of type I cryoglobulinaemia than of EMC. Rheumatoid factor is positive and complement levels are usually depressed in EMC. Although infection with Epstein-Barr virus and hepatitis B virus have been implicated in some cases; it now seems clear that most cases are due to chronic infection with hepatitis C virus (HCV).

15.10   E: Fingers are symmetrically involved during an attack

Characteristics	Primary Raynaud's phenomena	Secondary Raynaud's phenomena
Age (average)	30 years	> 50 years
Sex	Female	Male
Tissue damage	Absent	Digital ulcers, gangrene
Symmetry	Symmetrical attacks	Asymmetrical attacks
Capillary scope	- ve	+ ve
Auto-antibodies	- ve	+ ve
Associated disease	None	Scleroderma, SLE, other CTDs

15.11   D: Peripheral asymmetric oligoarthropathy
Peripheral oligoarthropathy is the most common and accounts for 35–40% of all cases of psoriatic arthritis. It usually comprises asymmetrical pattern of large and small limb joint involvement. Symmetric polyarthropathy resembling rheumatoid arthritis may occur in 20–30% of cases. Synovitis of the DIP joints of the hands, often in the joints adjacent to the affected nail, is almost pathognomonic of psoriatic arthropathy but constitutes < 10% of all cases. Arthritis mutilans is uncommon (< 5%). Psoriatic spondylitis accounts for approximately 20% of cases.

15.12   D: Elevated low density lipoprotein (LDL)
Antiphospholipid syndrome (APS) is characterised by thrombosis of arteries and veins, recurrent abortions and thrombocytopenia. It was first described in SLE, but has since been described in a wide range of autoimmune diseases associated with a variety of autoimmune autoantibodies, it can happen in isolation in the primary antiphospholipid syndrome. Antiphospholipid antibodies are immunoglobulins of the IgG and IgM class, which are directed against a negatively charged phospholipid molecule. The presence of antiphospholipid antibodies may be suggested by the presence of lupus anticoagulant, prolonged APTT, false positive VDRL and anticardiolipin antibodies measured by RIA or ELISA. Although there is increased risk of atherosclerosis and ischaemic heart disease in patients with SLE. Elevated LDL in is not a feature of primary APS.

15.13   A: Pulmonary hypertension is usually due to recurrent pulmonary embolism

Pulmonary hypertension is due to avascular obliterative mechanism, which is the hallmark of systemic sclerosis. Some patients have scleroderma visceral disease without cutaneous involvement (systemic sclerosis sine scleroderma). Trigeminal neuralgia and alveolar cell carcinoma are rare but recognised complications. The skin changes extend proximal to the MCP joints; a feature that helps to differentiate it from limited cutaneous sclerosis (CREST). In uncomplicated cases the ESR is typically within normal limits.

15.14   B: Tenosynovitis

In the early stages of the disease there is polyarthritis affecting the wrist and hand joints, but this soon gives place to monoarthritis when the disease is established. Synovial smear and culture are often negative. Synovial effusion often contains more than 100,000 leucocytes per cubic millimetre. In gonococcal arthritis there is a high frequency of associated tenosynovitis and skin rash (vesiculo-postural with erythematous base), both are characteristic. Resistance to penicillin is uncommon. The risk of dissemination is greater in females and is particularly high during menses, pregnancy, postpartum and in individuals with genetic deficiency in the terminal component of serum complement (C5, C6, C7 or C8). Episcleritis is a feature of seropositive inflammatory arthropathy.

15.15   B: Anti-ribonucleoprotein (anti-RNP antibody)

The patient's clinical features are highly suggestive of mixed connective tissue disease (MCTD). This diagnosis has been applied to a particular subset of patients with overlapping clinical features of lupus, scleroderma, and myositis. An immune response to U1-RNP is the additional defining serological feature of MCTD.

15.16   B: Addison's disease

Chondrocalcinosis is due to calcium pyrophosphate dihydrate (CPPD) crystal deposition. It can be an important clue to a number of systemic diseases, which include:

Hyperparathyroidism
Haemochromatosis
Hypothyroidism
Ochronosis
Hypophosphatasia
Hypomagnesaemia
Acromegaly

Wilson's disease

Complicates gout and rheumatoid arthritis

Addison's disease is not associated with increased incidence of crystal induced synovitis.

15.17   A: Spinal cord compression due to cervical myelopathy from atlanto-axial subluxation

This patient exhibits features of upper motor neurone signs affecting the upper and lower limbs. The most probable diagnosis is cervical myelopathy secondary to RA. The hallmark symptom of cervical myelopathy is weakness or stiffness in the legs and weakness or clumsiness of the hands. Loss of sphincter control or frank incontinence is rare; however, some patients may complain of slight hesitancy on urination. A characteristic physical finding of cervical myelopathy is hyperreflexia. Ankle clonus and Babinski's sign (pathological extension of the great toe elicited by stroking the foot) in the feet may also be revealed. Magnetic resonance imaging (MRI) of the cervical spine is the procedure of choice during the initial screening process of patients with suspected cervical myelopathy. In myasthenia gravis and disuse muscle atrophy Babinski's sign is negative. Subcutaneous rheumatoid nodules occur in 20–25% of patients. It is usually observed at areas subject to pressure, such as elbows, the occiput or the sacrum. The central nervous system is usually spared.

15.18   C: Ankylosing spondylitis

The character of the back pain implies inflammatory disease. Pain has persisted over three months. He noticed increasing back stiffness in the morning that improves during the day; the pain was probably so severe at night that it prompts him to get up and become mobile to reduce the symptoms. The above features suggest an inflammatory nature of the pain, most probably ankylosing spondylitis (AS). Patients with AS generally present with back pain that is worse after rest and improves with exercise. The onset is typically insidious in a male under 40 years of age. Sciatica is the symptomatic hallmark of clinically significant disc herniation. It presents as sharp or burning pain radiating down the posterior or lateral aspect of the leg to the ankle or foot (depending on the specific nerve root involved). The pain may be worsened by cough, Valsalva manoeuvre, or sneezing and is often accompanied by paraesthesia and numbness. 90% of mechanical causes of back pain last less than eight weeks. Spinal canal stenosis occurs in young people who have a congenitally narrowed lumbar spinal canal and also in elderly individuals with osteoarthritic spurring, chronic disc degeneration, and facet joint arthritis. The characteristic complaint is pain in the low back and gluteal region that is worsened by standing, walking, or other activities that cause spinal extension. Other characteristics are relief by rest, especially by sitting or lying down and flexing the spine and hips. Symptoms are often worsened by walking and relieved by sitting down and resting, they can mimic vascular insufficiency and are sometimes referred to as 'pseudo-claudication.' Back pain due to osteomyelitis is usually dull, often in conjunction with low-grade fever and spasm over the paraspinous muscles. Tenderness to percussion over the involved vertebrae is common, but fever is absent in up to 50% of cases. Malignant vertebral deposit often presents with severe deep seated pain that is worse at night and provoked by spine movement. In malignant and infectious cases of backache the disease process is rapidly progressive and serious compression fracture or an epidural abscess may ensue. The fact that this patient remained stable six months after presentation makes such a diagnosis unlikely.

Inflammatory vs mechanical back pain

Type	Mechanical	Inflammatory
Onset	Acute	Insidious
MS +	+++	
Exercise	Worse	Better
Radiation	L5 S1	Diffuse
Neurology	+ve	-ve

15.19 E: Increase the risk of clotting

Raloxifene is a selective oestrogen receptor modulator that produces both oestrogen-agonistic effects on bone and lipid metabolism and oestrogen-antagonistic effects on uterine endometrium and breast tissue. Raloxifene may have fewer side-effects than are typically observed with oestrogen therapy because of its tissue selectivity. The most common adverse effects of raloxifene are hot flushes and leg cramps. The drug is also associated with an increased risk of thromboembolic events. The beneficial oestrogenic activities of raloxifene include a lowering of total and low-density lipoprotein cholesterol levels and an augmentation of bone mineral density. Raloxifene reduces fracture risk at the spine but not at the hip. In women with a previous vertebral fracture, the magnitude of this reduction was dose-dependent and at least four times greater in women with no previous fracture. It does not raise triglyceride or HDL cholesterol levels. It does not have some of the side-effects of oestrogen, such as vaginal spotting (bleeding) and breast tenderness.

15.20   C: Polyarteritis nodosa

This patient presents with generalised features, abdominal pain, hypertension and mononeuritis. The raised ESR and polymorphonuclear leucocytosis consolidate the possibility of vasculitis, namely polyarteritis nodosa. The abdominal pain is highly suggestive of mesenteric ischaemia. Mononeuritis multiplex develops because of involvement of the vasa vasorum; it is reflected in the patient describing sudden loss of ability to dorsiflex his left great toe. Wegener's granulomatus and Churg-Strauss syndrome are commonly associated with pulmonary manifestations which are absent in this case and the chest X-ray is normal. SLE is more common in young females. Polymyalgia rheumatica presents with pain and stiffness in the shoulder and pelvic girdles, but hypertension and mononeuritis are not recognised features of the disorder.

15.21   B: Fibromyalgia syndrome

Fibromyalgia syndrome (FMS) is a commonly encountered syndrome characterised by diffuse persistent musculoskeletal pain, stiffness, tenderness, sleep disturbance and easy fatigability, affecting women predominantly from 30–60 years of age. The American College of Rheumatology (ACR) 1990 criteria for the classification of FMS allows positive identification of the syndrome which include:

1. History of widespread pain which has been present for at least three months.
2. Pain, on digital palpation, must be present in at least 11 of the following 8 tender point sites: *Occiput - Low cervical - Trapezius - Suprapinatus second rib - Lateral epicondyle - Gluteal - Greater trochanter - Knee.*

On physical examination, patients with primary FMS usually appear well with no obvious systemic illness or articular abnormalities. Tenderness is the feature that most readily allows separation of FMS from other disorders that produce widespread pain or fatigue as in chronic fatigue syndrome. Laboratory and radiological investigations in FMS are largely unrevealing and primarily useful in searching for the presence of concomitant disorders. Even among normal blood donors the incidence of a positive ANA is approximately 5% when the screening is done with a serum dilution of 1:40. The titre of the ANA test is usually >1:160 in the systemic connective tissue diseases. Certain rheumatic and non-rheumatic diseases can also mimic FMS, with similar complaints, mostly pain and fatigue, and must be considered and treated accordingly even when the FMS has been positively identified, examples include depression and hypothyroidism.

15.22 A: Diabetes mellitus is the most common cause

The mechanism that leads to the development of neuropathic joints is the impairment of proprioceptive and pain sensations which deprive the affected joint of the normal protective reactions that ordinarily modulate the forces of weight bearing and motion. It can be a complication of a variety of neurological disorders; diabetic neuropathy is the most common. Poliomyelitis is an acute viral illness that selectively destroys the motor neurones. It does not cause loss of sensation or proprioception and hence it is not a cause of neuropathic joints. The affected joint is grossly deformed with significant swelling reflecting severe degrees of destruction and disorganisation of the involved joints. The basic neurological lesion determines the distribution of the affected joint. In diabetic neuropathy, the changes are limited to the distal lower extremities and in syringomyelia the shoulder and elbows are most commonly affected. Total joint replacement has been attempted, but success has been limited and most consider this approach contraindicated.

15.23 B: Polyarteritis nodosa

ANCA can be detected in almost all patients with Wegener's granulomatosis. They are also found in 90% of cases of two related disorders with identical renal histological findings to Wegener's granulomatosis: microscopic polyangiitis, in which there are systemic symptoms that are not classic for Wegener's granulomatosis and idiopathic necrotising glomerulonephritis. Approximately 70% of patients with Churg-Strauss syndrome (allergic angiitis and granulomatosis) are also ANCA-positive. In contrast, ANCA are much less common in classic polyarteritis nodosa in which small and medium sized arteries are affected, occurring in approximately 20% of cases.

15.24 D: Eclampsia of pregnancy

The concentration of urate in plasma is determined by the balance between absorption and production of purines on the one hand and destruction and excretion on the other.

Causes include:

- Increased purine biosynthesis
- Lesch-Nyhan syndrome
- Glucose-6-phosphatase deficiency (von Gierke's disease)
- Increased nucleic acid turnover
- Haemolysis, polycythaemia rubra vera
- Reduced renal clearance
- Chronic renal failure, lead poisoning and diuretics
- Pre-eclampsia is characteristically associated with low uric acid levels

16: STATISTICS: ANSWERS AND EXPLANATIONS

16.1   C: The mean is higher than the median in positively skewed distributions

The mean is a good measure of central tendency for roughly symmetric distributions but can be misleading in skewed distributions since it can be greatly influenced by extreme scores. Therefore, other statistics such as the median may be more informative for distributions such as reaction time or family income that are frequently very skewed. For normal distributions, the mean is the most efficient and therefore the least subject to sample fluctuations of all measures of central tendency.

The median is the middle of a distribution (half the scores are above the median and half are below the median). The median is less sensitive to extreme scores than the mean and this makes it a better measure than the mean for highly skewed distributions. The median income is usually more informative than the mean income, for example, when there is an odd number of numbers, the median is simply the middle number when the numbers are arranged an order of magnitude. For example, the median of 2, 4, and 7 is 4.

When there is an even number of numbers, the median is the mean of the two middle numbers. Thus, the median of the numbers 2, 4, 7, 12 is $(4+7)/2 = 5.5$.

The mean, median, and mode are equal in symmetric distributions. The mean is higher than the median in positively skewed distributions and lower than the median in negatively skewed distributions.

The mode is the most frequently occurring score in a distribution and is used as a measure of central tendency. The advantage of the mode as a measure of central tendency is that its meaning is obvious. Further, it is the only measure of central tendency that can be used with nominal data.

The mode is greatly subject to sample fluctuations and is therefore not recommended to be used as the only measure of central tendency. A further disadvantage of the mode is that many distributions have more than one mode. These distributions are called 'multimodal.'

16.2   C: For every 5 who smoke, 1 has the disease

The odds in a given group (in this case smokers) is defined as the number with disease/number without disease. Since odds = ¼ i.e. for every 1 smoker with the disease 4 do not have the disease, for every 5 that smoke 1 has the disease and C is correct.

16.3   C: Nothing conclusive can be said, a larger study is needed
Because 0/31 have serious side-effects does not mean that no infants ever will, so the drug has not been shown to be safe (A, B, D and E are incorrect). If 3% of infants were to have serious side-effects from taking the drug, then we would only expect to get 1 in a sample of 30 and it would not be that surprising to get none. A larger study needs to be done to try and get a more precise estimate of the percentage who will suffer serious side-effects hopefully discounting larger percentages.

**16.4   B: We are approximately 95% confident that the population
          average blood pressure for Asian women lies in the interval
          (49, 51)**
Approximately 95% will have blood pressures in the range (mean ± 2sd) = (50 ± 2(5)) = (50 ± 10) = (40, 60) so A is incorrect.
2.5% will have blood pressures below 40 (D is incorrect).
A 95% confidence interval for average blood pressure is given by (mean ± 2se) = (50 ± 2 (5)) = (50 ± 1) = (49, 51), so B is correct. (Although we are 95% confident that the mean lies in this range it may not and E is incorrect.)

16.5   E: Smaller than the standard deviation
Standard error = standard deviation/% (sample size). In this case, sd = 5/%(100) =5/10=0.5. The standard error is, by definition, always smaller than the standard deviation, hence E is correct.

REVISION CHECKLIST FOR THE MRCP 1 EXAM

Numbers in brackets indicate relative frequency of topics.

BASIC SCIENCES
Physiology
➢ Changes in pregnancy (2)
➢ Haemoglobin function
➢ Physiology of bone
➢ Aetiology of oedema

Pathology
➢ Amyloid plaques
➢ Apoptosis

Hormone and mediator biochemistry
➢ Atrial natriuretic peptides (4)
➢ Insulin/insulin resistance (3)
➢ Nitric oxide (3)
➢ Angiotensin (2)
➢ Neurotransmitters (2)
➢ Prostacyclin (2)
➢ Adenosine
➢ ADH
➢ Aldosterone
➢ H2 receptors
➢ Somatostatin
➢ Steroid receptors

Miscellaneous
➢ Organelles with DNA (2)
➢ Apolipoproteins
➢ Alpha$_1$-antitrypsin
➢ Oncogenes

CARDIOLOGY
Valvular heart disease
➢ Heart sounds (4)
➢ Mitral stenosis (3)
➢ Valve lesions/murmurs (3)
➢ Antibiotic prophylaxis
➢ Catheterisation data
➢ Mitral valve prolapse

Arrhythmias
➢ Wolff-Parkinson-White/SVT (6)
➢ Atrial fibrillation (3)
➢ Ventricular tachycardia (3)
➢ LBBB (2)
➢ Prolonged Q-T (2)
➢ Torsades des pointes

Pericardial disease
➢ Constrictive pericarditis (7)
➢ Cardiac tamponade (1)
➢ Pericardial effusion
➢ *IHD/heart muscle disease*
➢ Myocardial infarction (6)
➢ Cardiomyopathy (3)
➢ Left ventricular failure (2)
➢ Unstable angina (2)
➢ Coronary bypass surgery
➢ Left ventricular hypertrophy
➢ Signs underlying heart disease

Congenital heart disease
➢ Cyanotic heart disease/ Eisenmenger's (4)
➢ ASD (3)
➢ Patent ductus arteriosus
➢ VSD

Large vessel disease
➢ Pulmonary embolus (4)
➢ Aortic dissection (3)
➢ Pulmonary hypertension (3)

Miscellaneous
➢ Cannon "a" waves in JVP (4)
➢ Alcohol and the heart (3)
➢ Carotid body/cardiac sympathetics (2)
➢ Coronary circulation
➢ Left atrial myxoma

DERMATOLOGY
Specific skin lesions
➢ Erythema multiforme (2)
➢ Psoriasis (2)
➢ Alopecia areata
➢ Erythema nodosum
➢ Papular rash
➢ Purpura

Systemic manifestations
➢ Pruritus (3)
➢ Photosensitivity (2)
➢ Skin manifestations of systemic disease

Miscellaneous
- ➤ Foot ulcers
- ➤ Lesions on limbs

ENDOCRINOLOGY
Diabetes and glycaemic control
- ➤ Diabetes (11)
- ➤ Hypoglycaemia (4)
- ➤ Glycosylated haemoglobin
- ➤ Hepatic gluconeogenesis
- ➤ Insulinoma

Adrenal disease
- ➤ Cushing's syndrome (8)
- ➤ Addison's disease (4)
- ➤ Congenital adrenal hyperplasia (4)
- ➤ ACTH action

Thyroid disease
- ➤ Thyroxine action/metabolism TFTs (6)
- ➤ Thyroid cancer/nodule (3)
- ➤ Graves'disease/exophthalmos (2)
- ➤ Hypothyroidism (2)

Parathyroid disease
- ➤ PTH/hyperparathyroidism (4)
- ➤ Calcitonin (2)

Pituitary disease
- ➤ Acromegaly (5)
- ➤ Chromophobe adenoma (2)
- ➤ Hyperprolactinaemia (2)
- ➤ Hypopituitarism
- ➤ Pituitary hormones

Miscellaneous
- ➤ Polycystic ovary syndrome/infertility (4)
- ➤ SIADH (3)
- ➤ Short stature
- ➤ Weight gain/Prader-Willi Syndrome (2)
- ➤ Endocrine changes in anorexia
- ➤ Hirsutism
- ➤ Hormone physiology (including pregnancy)
- ➤ Sweating

GASTROENTEROLOGY
Liver disease
- ➤ Chronic liver disease (2)
- ➤ Jaundice (4)
- ➤ Primary biliary cirrhosis (4)
- ➤ Gilbert's syndrome (2)
- ➤ Hepatic mass/sub-phrenic abscess (2)
- ➤ Alcohol & liver
- ➤ Portal vein thrombosis

Small bowel disease/Malabsorption
- ➤ Coeliac disease (7)
- ➤ Malabsorption/protein-losing enteropathy (4)
- ➤ Cholera toxin/gastroenteritis (3)
- ➤ Carcinoid syndrome
- ➤ Whipple's disease
  (see also 'Crohn's disease' below)

Large bowel disorders
- ➤ Crohn's disease (6)
- ➤ Ulcerative colitis/colonic carcinoma (6)
- ➤ Irritable bowel syndrome (3)
- ➤ Diarrhoea (2)
- ➤ Inflammatory bowel disease – general (2)
- ➤ Pseudomembranous colitis

Oesophageal disease
- ➤ Gastro-oesophageal reflux/tests (4)
- ➤ Achalasia (3)
- ➤ Dysphagia/oesophageal tumour (2)
- ➤ Oesophageal chest pain

Stomach and pancreas
- ➤ Acute pancreatitis (4)
- ➤ Gastric acid secretion (2)
- ➤ Persistent vomiting
- ➤ Stomach cancer

Miscellaneous
- ➤ GI tract bleeding (4)
- ➤ Abdominal X-ray
- ➤ GI hormones
- ➤ Physiology of absorption
- ➤ Recurrent abdominal pain

GENETICS
Syndromes
➤ Klinefelter's syndrome (4)
➤ Turner's syndrome (2)
➤ Down's syndrome (2)

Modes of inheritance
➤ X-linked conditions (2)
➤ Autosomal recessive (2)
➤ Autosomal dominant
➤ Genetic anticipation
➤ Inheritance patterns (various)

Miscellaneous
➤ Abnormal karyotype (4)
➤ Chorionic villous sampling
➤ Chorionic defects

HAEMATOLOGY
Red cell physiology and anaemias
➤ Iron deficiency/metabolism/ therapy (4)
➤ Macrocytosis/pernicious anaemia (4)
➤ Folate deficiency (3)
➤ Basophilia (2)
➤ Erythropoiesis/Hb physiology (2)
➤ Haem biosynthesis (2)
➤ Sideroblastic anaemia (2)
➤ Aplastic anaemia
➤ Investigation of anaemia
➤ Vitamin B12 metabolism

Haemolytic anaemia
➤ Haemolytic anaemia (7)
➤ Sickle cell/Haemoglobinopathy (7)
➤ Hereditary spherocytosis (2)
➤ Reticulocytosis (2)
➤ G-6-PD deficiency
➤ Haemolytic-uraemic syndrome
➤ Intravascular haemolysis

Bleeding disorders
➤ Thrombocytopaenia (2)
➤ Haemophilia (2)
➤ Bleeding time
➤ Fresh frozen plasma
➤ Von Willebrand's disease

Haematological malignancy
➤ Hodgkin's/Non-Hodgkin's lymphoma (5)
➤ Leukaemia (2)
➤ Pancytopenia/splenomegaly (5)
➤ Polycythaemia (2)

Miscellaneous
➤ Hyposplenism (2)
➤ Methaemoglobinaemia (2)
➤ Neutropaenia (2)
➤ Thrombocytosis (2)
➤ Bone infarction
➤ Bone marrow test
➤ Eosinophilia
➤ Hyperuricaemia and haematological disease
  (see also Metabolic Disease)
➤ Paroxysmal nocturnal haemoglobinuria

IMMUNOLOGY
Cytokines
➤ Tumour necrosis factor (3)
➤ Interferon (2)
➤ Inflammatory mediators (general)
➤ Leukotrienes

Cellular immunity
➤ T lymphocytes/deficiency (5)
➤ Cell-mediated immunity (2)

Immunoglobulins/autoimmunity
➤ IgA/IgE/IgG (4)
➤ Autoimmune disease/ANCA (2)
➤ Hypogammaglobulinaemia (2)
➤ Monoclonal gammopathy (2)
➤ Tissue receptor antibodies (2)
➤ Circulating immune complexes
➤ Precipitating antibodies in diagnosis

Miscellaneous
➤ Complement/CH_{50} (2)
➤ Angioneurotic oedema (2)
➤ Hypersensitivity reactions (2)
➤ Mast cells
➤ Polymerase chain reaction
➤ Post-splenectomy
➤ Transplant rejection

INFECTIOUS DISEASES
Viral Infections
➣ Hepatitis (6)
➣ Infectious mononucleosis (6)
➣ Chickenpox/measles/mumps (5)
➣ AIDS/HIV (4)
➣ Adenovirus
➣ Genital herpes
➣ Parvovirus

Bacterial Infections
➣ Venereal disease (8)
➣ Brucellosis (4)
➣ TB/BCG (4)
➣ Tetanus (4)
➣ Toxoplasmosis (4)
➣ Typhoid/cholera (4)
➣ Bacteroides
➣ *Haemophilus influenza*
➣ *Helicobacter pylori*
➣ Lyme disease
➣ Meningitis
➣ Pneumonia
➣ Staphylococcus

Routes of infection
➣ Transmission by insect bite (3)
➣ Faecal-oral transmission (2)

Tropical and protozoal infections
➣ Malaria (9)
➣ Tropical fever/splenomegaly (2)
➣ Giardiasis
➣ *Pneumocystis carinii*
➣ Schistosomiasis
Miscellaneous
➣ *Chlamydia trachomatis* (2)
➣ Other infections/diarrhoea (2)
➣ Chronic infection and anaemia
➣ Infections and eosinophilia
➣ Prion disease

METABOLIC DISEASE
Overdose and poisoning
➣ Carbon monoxide/other poisoning (5)
➣ Salicylate/paracetamol overdose (4)
➣ Tricyclic/theophylline overdose (4)
➣ Excess alcohol (2)
➣ Iron toxicity

Disorders of bone
➣ Osteoporosis (4)
➣ Vitamin D metabolism (4)
➣ Achondroplasia
➣ Calcium homeostasis
➣ Increased alkaline phosphatase
➣ Increased prostate-specific antigen
➣ Paget's disease

Disorders of acid/base and electrolytes
➣ Hyper/hypokalaemia (4)
➣ Alkalosis/vomiting (3)
➣ Hypomagnesaemia (3)
➣ Hyponatraemia/chloride depletion (2)
➣ Hypophosphataemia (2)
➣ Hypercalcaemia
➣ Hypernatraemia
➣ Polydipsia

Inherited metabolic disorders
➣ Hypercholesterolaemia (2)
➣ Wilson's disease (2)
➣ Alpha$_1$-antitrypsin deficiency (*see also Basic Science*)
➣ Homocystinuria
➣ Malignant neuroleptic syndrome

Miscellaneous
➣ Hypothermia (2)
➣ Hypercarotenemia
➣ Hyperuricaemia
➣ Kwashiorkor
➣ Marfan's syndrome
➣ Obesity
➣ Thiamine deficiency

NEPHROLOGY
Nephrotic syndrome/related glomeru-lonephritis
➣ Nephrotic syndrome (9)
➣ Membranous glomerulonephritis (4)
➣ Minimal Change disease (4)
➣ Hypocomplementaemia & glomeru-lonephritis (2)
➣ Renal vein thrombosis (2)
➣ Acute glomerulonephritis
➣ SLE nephritis

Renal failure
➢ Acute renal failure (4)
➢ Acute versus chronic (3)
➢ Chronic renal failure (3)
➢ Haemolytic-uraemic syndrome (2)
➢ Rhabdomyolysis (2)
➢ Anaemia in renal failure
➢ Contrast nephropathy

Urinary abnormalities
➢ Macroscopic haematuria (2)
➢ Discolouration of the urine
➢ Nocturia
➢ Polyuria

Basic renal physiology
➢ Normal renal physiology/ function (6)
➢ Water excretion/urinary concentration (2)
➢ Serum creatinine

Miscellaneous
➢ Distal renal tubular acidosis (5)
➢ Renal papillary necrosis (4)
➢ Diabetic nephropathy (3)
➢ Analgesic nephropathy
➢ Polycystic kidney disease
➢ Renal calculi
➢ Renal osteodystrophy
➢ Retroperitoneal fibrosis
➢ Steroid therapy in renal disease

NEUROLOGY
Abnormalities of brain & cerebral circulation
➢ Dementia/Alzheimer's (5)
➢ Transient ischaemic attacks (4)
➢ Benign intracranial hypertension/brain tumour (3)
➢ Head injury (3)
➢ Lateral medullary/circulatory syndromes (3)
➢ Subdural haematoma (3)
➢ Encephalitis (2)
➢ Parietal lobe/frontal cortical lesions (2)
➢ Temporal lobe epilepsy (2)
➢ Amnesia
➢ Central pontine myelinolysis

➢ Cerebral abscess
➢ Creutzfeldt-Jakob disease
➢ EEG
➢ Intracranial calcification
➢ Midbrain (Parinaud's) syndrome
➢ Normal pressure hydrocephalus
➢ Wernicke's encephalopathy

Spinal cord and peripheral nerve anatomy & lesions
➢ Innervation of specific muscles (4)
➢ Median nerve/brachial plexus (3)
➢ Posterior nerve root/spinal ganglia lesions (3)
➢ Dorsal interosseous nerve (2)
➢ Guillain-Barré (2)
➢ Pyramidal tracts/posterior column pathways (2)
➢ Sciatic nerve lesion (2)
➢ Autonomic spondylosis
➢ Cervical spondylosis
➢ Motor neuron disease
➢ Paraesthesia
➢ Spinal cord lesions

Cranial nerve anatomy & lesions
➢ Facial nerve (6)
➢ Cranial nerve lesions (5)
➢ Third nerve palsy/pupillary reflex (3)
➢ Bulbar palsy
➢ Internuclear ophthalmoplegia
➢ 4th nerve palsy

Dyskinesias
➢ Ataxia (2)
➢ Benign essential tremor (2)
➢ Dyskinesia
➢ Parkinson's disease

Muscular disorders
➢ Duchenne muscular dystrophy (4)
➢ Myotonic dystrophy (2)
➢ Myaesthenia gravis

Miscellaneous
➢ Multiple sclerosis (5)
➢ Headache/migraine (4)
➢ Lumbar puncture/CSF (3)
➢ Nystagmus (3)
➢ Pseudofits (2)

➢ Vertigo/dysarthria (2)
➢ CNS involvement in AIDS

PHARMACOLOGY
Interactions/dose adjustment
➢ Drug interactions (10)
➢ Pregnancy/breast feeding (7)
➢ Adverse effects - general (4)
➢ Dose adjustment in renal failure (3)
➢ Drugs in porphyria
➢ Polymorphism of drug metabolism

Specific side-effects of drugs
➢ Asthma exacerbation (2)
➢ Causing hypothyroidism (2)
➢ Gynaecomastia/
  hyperprolactinaemia (2)
➢ Hepatic enzyme inducers
➢ Hypokalaemia
➢ Aggravation of skin disorders
➢ Convulsions
➢ Haemolytic anaemia

Fundamental pharmacology
➢ Mechanisms of drug/antibiotic
  action (2)

Most frequently considered individual agents
➢ Antipsychotics/depressants (5)
➢ ACE inhibitors (4)
➢ Amiodarone (4)
➢ Thiazides (4)
➢ Anti-convulsants (3)
➢ Digoxin (3)
➢ Lithium (3)
➢ Sulphasalazine (2)
➢ Metronidazole
➢ Radio-iodine

Other 'topical' agents
➢ Azidothymidine (AZT)
➢ Cimetidine
➢ Gentamicin
➢ Griseofulvin
➢ HMG Co-A reductase inhibitor
➢ L-dopa
➢ Metronidazole
➢ Penicillamine
➢ Retinoic acid
➢ Warfarin

PSYCHIATRY
Psychotic disorders
➢ Schizophrenia (8)
➢ Depression (7)
➢ Mania (6)
➢ Hallucinations/delusions (3)

Anxiety states/compulsive disorders
➢ Neurosis/psychogenic/ conversion
  disorders (5)
➢ Obsessional/compulsive disorders
  (5)
➢ Panic attack

Eating disorders
➢ Anorexia nervosa (9)
➢ Bulimia (2)

Other cognitive disorders
➢ Differentiation of dementia and
  depression (3)
➢ Acute confusional state (2)

Miscellaneous
➢ Psychiatric manifestations of organic
  disease (6)
➢ Alcohol dependency (3)
➢ Insomnia (2)
➢ Narcolepsy (2)
➢ Endocrine causes of psychiatric dis-
  ease
➢ Psychiatric manifestations in adoles-
  cence

RESPIRATORY DISEASE
Respiratory infections
➢ Pneumonia (7)
➢ Broncho-pulmonary aspergillosis (3)
➢ Acute bronchiolitis
➢ Psittacosis
➢ Viral infections

Lung cancer
➢ Bronchial carcinoma (5)
➢ Surgery for cancer (3)
➢ Pancoast's tumour
➢ Small cell cancer

Pulmonary physiology
- ➤ Lung function tests (4)
- ➤ Normal physiology (3)
- ➤ Transfer factor (2)
- ➤ Forced hyperventilation

End-stage lung disease
- ➤ Respiratory failure (4)
- ➤ Long-term oxygen

Interstitial lung disease/fibrosis
- ➤ Extrinsic allergic alveolitis (6)
- ➤ Bronchiectasis (4)
- ➤ ARDS (3)
- ➤ Sarcoidosis (3)
- ➤ Emphysema (2)
- ➤ Fibrosing alveolitis (2)
- ➤ Pulmonary fibrosis (2)
- ➤ Asbestosis
- ➤ Cystic fibrosis

Miscellaneous
- ➤ Asthma (5)
- ➤ Sleep-apnoea syndrome (5)
- ➤ Autoimmune disease and lung (3)
- ➤ Abnormal chest X-ray (2)
- ➤ Lung cavitation
- ➤ Pulmonary eosinophilia

RHEUMATOLOGY
Auto-immune disease
- ➤ Rheumatoid arthritis (7)
- ➤ SLE (7)
- ➤ Wegener's granulomatosis (2)

Other vasculitides
- ➤ Polymyalgia rheumatica (4)
- ➤ Cranial arteritis
- ➤ Vasculitic disease

Other arthritides
- ➤ Reiter's syndrome (3)
- ➤ Ankylosing spondylitis/HLA B27 (2)
- ➤ Arthralgia (2)
- ➤ Behçet's disease (2)
- ➤ Arthropathy (general)
- ➤ Hypertrophic osteo-arthropathy
- ➤ Osteoarthritis
- ➤ Pseudogout

Miscellaneous
- ➤ Anti-phospholipid syndrome (3)
- ➤ Digital gangrene
- ➤ Peri-articular calcification
- ➤ Systemic sclerosis

STATISTICS
Statistical populations
- ➤ Normal distribution (4)
- ➤ Standard deviation (3)
- ➤ Skewed distribution

Tests of significance
- ➤ Significance test (6)
- ➤ Chi-square test
- ➤ Type I and II errors
- ➤ Skewed distribution

Miscellaneous
- ➤ Specificity of clinical trials (2)

REVISION INDEX

The numbers in this index refer to the chapter and question number. The word shown may not always be used in the question but may appear in the explanatory answer.

BE PREPARED FOR THE NEW MRCP 1 EXAM WITH PASTEST

EXAM FORMAT

From May 2002 the MRCP 1 examination will change in format. There will be two papers, each of two and a half hours' duration.

- First paper: 60 multiple true/false questions with 300 individual items
- Second paper: 100 multiple choice 'best of five' questions (there is one best answer from five)
- Negative marking will be discontinued
- The examination will be criterion referenced: i.e there will be a pre-determined pass mark

(See the Royal College of Physicians' Web Site www.rcplondon.ac.uk)

HOW PASTEST CAN HELP YOU TO PREPARE

At PasTest we have been preparing for the new exam paper for over 18 months. We have compiled a comprehensive bank of new questions across all specialties to ensure that candidates attending our courses in Spring 2002 will receive teaching on the new format questions.

NEW BOOKS

New titles have been developed so that all candidates can feel confident that they have prepared both for the new exam paper and the old-style multiple true/false paper.

SEE OVER FOR DETAILS OF OUR MRCP1 TITLES

NEW PASTEST BOOKS FOR MRCP PART 1

MRCP 1 Multiple True/False Revision Book- Kalra   Dec 2001 £24.95
This book brings together 600 PasTest multiple true/false questions into one volume. The book is split into subjects but also contains a practice exam so that you can test your knowledge. Again, detailed teaching notes are provided.

MRCP 1 Pocket Book Series   Nov 2001 £11.95 each
A series of four new pocket books covering all major specialties. Each book will contain an equal mix of old and new format questions so that you can tailor your revision to concentrate on specific subjects.

Book 1:   Cardiology, Respiratory, Haematology

Book 2:   Neurology, Psychiatry, Basic Sciences

Book 3:   Gastroenterology, Endocrinology, Nephrology

Book 4:   Clinical Pharmacology, infectious Diseases, Rheumatology, Immunology

PASTEST BOOKS FOR MRCP PART 1

Essential Revision Notes for MRCP Revised Edition
A definitive guide to revision for the MRCP examination. 19 chapters of informative material necessary to gain a successful exam result.

Explanations to the RCP 1997 Past Papers
180 answers and teaching notes to the Royal College of Physicians book of MCQs from the MRCP Part 1 1997 Examinations.

Explanations to the RCP 1990 Past Papers
180 answers and teaching notes to the Royal College of Physicians book of MCQs from the MRCP Part 1 1990 Examinations.

MRCP Part 1 MCQs with Key Topic Summaries 2nd edition
200 MCQs with comprehensive key topic summaries bridging the gap between standard MCQ books and textbooks.

MRCP Part 1 MCQs in Basic Sciences
300 exam-based MCQs focusing on basic sciences, with answers and teaching notes.

PASTEST –
DEDICATED TO YOUR SUCCESS

PasTest has been publishing books for doctors for over 25 years. Our extensive experience means that we are always one step ahead when it comes to knowledge of current trends and content of the Royal College exams.

We use only the best authors and lecturers, many of whom are Consultants and Royal College Examiners, which enables us to tailor our books and courses to meet your revision needs. We incorporate feedback from candidates to ensure that our books are continually improved.

This commitment to quality ensures that students who buy a PasTest book or attend a PasTest course achieve successful exam results.

100% Money Back Guarantee

We're sure you will find our study books invaluable, but in the unlikely event that you are not entirely happy, we will give you your money back – guaranteed.

Delivery to your Door

With a busy lifestyle, nobody enjoys walking to the shops for something that may or may not be in stock. Let us take the hassle and deliver direct to your door. We will despatch your book within 24 hours of receiving your order. We also offer free delivery on books for medical students to UK addresses.